Blood on whose hands?

✳

WOMEN'S COALITION AGAINST FAMILY VIOLENCE

This book is dedicated to all of the women and children whose lives were ended by the men in their lives, and to the eventual elimination of all forms of violence by men towards women and children.

Blood on whose hands?

The killing of women & children in domestic homicides

WOMEN'S COALITION AGAINST FAMILY VIOLENCE

Funded by the

Victorian
WOMEN'S TRUST
making a difference

First published 1994.

The Women's Coalition Against Family Violence is committed to the broad dissemination of the information contained in this book for the purposes of challenging the political and social conditions that allow domestic violence and domestic murder to continue.

Anyone using material from this book should make acknowledgment of the book, in recognition of the efforts made by so many women and the courage of surviving family members and friends.

National Library of Australia Cataloguing-in-Publication data:

Blood on whose hands?

ISBN 0 646 17924 1
1. Family violence — Victoria. 2. Family violence — Law and legislation — Victoria. 3. Homicides — Victoria. 4. Women — Crimes against — Victoria. 5. Children — Crimes against — Victoria.
I. Women's Coalition Against Family Violence.

364.15209945

LAW

Designed and typeset by: Susan Miller Graphic Design.
Set in 11.5/12.5 pt Garamond.
Edited by: Amanda Brett, Lynn Buchanan.
Printed by: Arena Printing and Publishing,
            35 Argyle Street, Fitzroy, Vic., 3065
Cover painting: Jude Robinson — "…female life surviving the barren hills and the prickliness of a juicy but harsh cactus world…"
Painting photographed by Ian Jones.

Contents

✳

How the book came about

＊

The **Women's Coalition Against Family Violence** is a community-based women's network. It was formed in 1987 to work towards changing the current situation in which many women and children are abused on a daily basis by their partners, ex-partners and fathers, and in which some women and children are murdered. The coalition comprises a range of women from community legal centres, community health services, refuges, sexual assault services and neighbourhood houses, and interested individuals.

In the few years after the coalition began community education work to raise the community's understanding of domestic violence and domestic murder, a number of family members of women and children who had been murdered made contact with us. To bring the issues to the attention of the public and the media, the coalition organised an event in May 1989 to commemorate the deaths of the many women and children who have been murdered by their partners, ex-partners and fathers.

While organising the commemoration, the coalition researched the media coverage of murders (or lack thereof) and met with family members and friends who survived the murdered women and children. At the commemoration, family members were able to tell the stories that had been ignored or misrepresented throughout the legal process and in the media.

They emphasised the long history of violence preceding the murders of the women and children. They said that almost without exception the response of the police was inadequate and inappropriate in the light of the history of domestic violence which led up to the murders, and they expressed a range of criticisms of the legal profession and the courts in their dealings with witnesses, the dead women and children and the men who had killed them.

Following the Domestic Murders Commemoration, the coalition, in conjunction with family members and friends of the murdered women and children, decided to undertake research aimed at documenting and publicising the reality and extent of domestic violence that precedes domestic murder. As much as possible, we have attempted to bring to the fore the stories of the murdered women and children, as told to us by their friends and families.

These accounts highlight the extent of institutional and community inaction towards, and therefore complicity in, domestic violence. They also make it clear that the killings were not merely inexplicable or aberrant occurrences, and that they did not occur as a result of drunkenness, stress, conflict, madness, "provocation" or any of the many other ostensible reasons we so frequently hear from the courts and the media. Rather, the killings were the end point of strategies used by men to control and dominate their wives, girlfriends, ex-partners and children.

In addition to trying to put forward the stories of the women and children, we have documented and analysed a range of other materials to illuminate the context of domestic murders and the response of the community, police, legal system and media to these murders. We held many meetings with groups and individuals who could give us information about men's violence against women and children. We read and analysed a range of secondary, theoretical and factual information, relating both to domestic violence and to women's social and economic status.

We researched and incorporated material gathered from the Victorian Coroner's Court files, which contain transcripts of inquest proceedings and findings and inquest briefs, which include statements of witnesses, police reports and experts' evidence. We researched the files of the Department of Public Prosecutions, which include committal and Supreme Court trial transcripts, together with police statements, medical evidence and statements by witnesses. We also researched the homicide squad's murders registration book, which gives the locations, times and days of the murders, occupations of those involved, accounts of what is thought to have happened and possible motives and, when known, the charges, convictions and sentences. Media clippings were also collected and analysed.

As we waded through mountains of papers and documents, the uniform absence of any attempt to provide an account of the victim's life and the context and history of violence which preceded the murder was striking. Throughout the entire process, from initial police investigations through to court trials and media reporting, we witnessed the systematic silencing and marginalising of the experiences of the dead women and children, and the relentless focus on attempting to justify or explain away the killer's actions. It was the victim, and not the offender whom we saw being described as inadequate, demanding, aggressive and provocative. It was she, in her absence, who was being assessed, judged, treated and punished. Judicial pronouncements echoed sexist, racist and class-based assumptions, as they attempted to frame the killer's actions as understandable, if not forgivable. These official versions, with their claims to neutrality and objectivity, obscure the power relationships underpinning domestic violence and murder, resulting in further victimisation and negation of the murdered woman or child.

In this book we have interwoven detailed material relating to a group of nine women and three children with material relating to other murdered women and children, as well as information about the social context in which such murders occur. Specifically, we document the social and economic context of these murders, including information relating to financial and social status and consequent options, and the policies and practices of the police, the legal system and the media. By so doing, we hope to make it clear that social change is urgently required to end the oppression and murder of women and children.

In publishing these accounts there have been many difficulties. A number of people interviewed did not want us to include any direct information about the person who was killed, usually for fear of violent repercussions, and consequently, those women and children have not been profiled in this report. Nevertheless, the contributions and insights of their families and friends have enriched this book considerably.

In the cases of the nine women and three children which we present in detail, some surviving family members and friends felt strongly that they wanted the whole story told, including the names of the murdered women and children and those who killed them. Others were afraid of further abuse by the killer. Some have already received threats to their lives and safety by these men. Some were torn between wanting the story to be told and respecting the wishes of other members of their family who didn't want any publicity. Many family members spoke of protecting the safety and privacy of surviving children, and they spoke movingly of the pain and torment that these children have experienced, many of them having seen their mother murdered in front of them, and some living in the custody of the man who killed her.

We have changed the names of some of those involved so that they cannot be easily identified. Some of the names and dates have been changed. Those that have been are not distinguished from those that have not.

We are grateful for the contribution of all who have participated in our research. We recognise that for those who have shared with us the lives of their friends and loved ones, who are not here to tell us themselves, that this has opened painful memories. We hope that this project will go some way towards shifting community attitudes and the detrimental responses of the legal system, and that it will bring about the social change that is necessary in order to prevent further violence and deaths.

An enormous amount of research and writing has been done about women's social and economic position in society and this project draws on some of that work. We also wish to acknowledge the contribution of all women who have worked hard to force these issues into the public consciousness and onto the political agenda. This book is part of our contribution to this ongoing work.

Thanks

✳

We would like to thank the Victorian Women's Trust for providing the funds to carry out and publish this project. With their assistance we were able to employ two part-time researchers who went through the material, spoke to the family members and friends and commenced the initial drafts. The project was much bigger than was originally anticipated and an enormous amount of voluntary time has been contributed by members of the steering group as well as some paid time and resources by some of the community organisations to which our members belong.

We would like to thank the Victorian Women's Trust and the other organisations and individuals who donated time and resources, as well as the families and friends we interviewed, for their commitment and patience in awaiting this, the final result.

The names of all who have contributed are listed below, except for those family and friends who did not wish to be named.

Coalition Against Family Violence

Carmel Boyce, Magenta Butler, Julia Cabassi, Jeanette Carrison, Ariel Couchman, Mary Danckert, Maria Dimopoulos, Amanda George, Judy Gibson, Cathy Hennenberg, Sabra

Lazarus, Kath McCarthy, Jude McCulloch, Chris Momot, Michele Old, Liz Orr, Liz Short, Petrina Smith, Tess Snowball.

Researchers, writers and editors

Carmel Boyce, Magenta Butler, Julia Cabassi, Ariel Couchman, Mary Danckert, Maria Dimopoulos, Amanda George, Sabra Lazarus, Kath McCarthy, Liz Short, Petrina Smith.

Design

Susan Miller Graphic Design

Organisations

Coburg Brunswick Community Legal and Financial Counselling Centre, Domestic Violence and Incest Resource Centre, Essendon Community Legal Centre, Women's Information Referral Exchange, Federation of Community Legal Centres, Women's Refuge Referral Service, Caroline Lodge, Barwon Women's Refuge, Zelda's Place, Mountain Women's Refuge, Women's Health Service for the West, Valerie House, Robinson House, Women's Liberation Halfway House, Refuge Ethnic Workers Program, Cooroonya House, Southern Halfway House, Women's Resource Information and Support Centre, Kara House, Sheila West Women's Refuge, Brenda House, Maroondah Halfway House, Nydia, Emma House, Kilvington House, Latrobe Women's Refuge, Women Against Rough Situations, Morgana Women's Refuge, Geelong Salvation Army Kywong, Geelong Trades Hall Council, Director of Public Prosecutions, Victorian Homicide Squad, Community Education Task Force on Family Violence, Federated Clerks Union, Boomerang Club, Mallesons Stephen Jaques Solicitors.

Other Individuals

Renata Alexander, Inspector Noel Ashby, Christine Atieno, Slavka Badar, June Baker, Rhonda Baker, Rose Banaghan-Sesta, Greta Bird, Karen Bird, Philip Cleary, Jennifer Coate, Stephen Eastop, Jenny Florence, Ian Freckleton, Bruce Gardner, Robyn Greensill, Emma King, Lillian Leider, Sue Macgregor, Melba Marginson, Robert Morsillo, Bronwyn Naylor, David Neal, Sati Ozbek, Kate Robinson, Marie Rowan, Kirsty Rowe, Luna Ruiz, Jocelynne Scutt, Sonya Tremellen, Domenica Vadala, Linda Vella, Rosemary Wearing, Rosemary West, Jacky Whittaker, Barb Younger.

Introduction

✳

Each year in Victoria between thirty and forty women and children are killed by their husbands, de factos, boyfriends, ex-partners, fathers and sons.[1] By far the largest category of reported homicides consists of those classified as "domestic", with men constituting the overwhelming majority of offenders, and women and children the overwhelming majority of victims.[2]

In its 1991 homicide report, the Victorian Law Reform Commission classified domestic homicides as homicides "where victim and offender were living in or intimately connected with the same household".[3] This includes separated spouses. We have expanded this definition to include intimate relationships where the parties have not lived together; however, our focus is on women and children, not men, as the victims of domestic murder because it is they who are most likely to be murdered. It is they who are overwhelmingly murdered by the men in their lives after a history of violence inflicted on them by these men. Where women have killed their male partners, it is well documented that it is likely to have been as a result of a long history of being victimised by them.[4]

When we use the term *domestic violence* we are referring to the gamut of abuse, coercion and control — whether it be psychological abuse, physical or sexual assault, financial deprivation and control, threats, control of movements, other forms of social abuse and other actions or behaviours which cause physical, sexual or psychological damage or cause women and children to live in fear. The most extreme form of this violence is murder.

Overwhelmingly, violence and abuse in the domestic setting is committed by men against women and children.[5] A woman is many times more likely to be assaulted by her partner or ex-partner than by anyone else, and statistics show that being at home with a male partner is the most unsafe place for a woman to be.[6] Women are many times more likely to be murdered by their male partners or ex-partners than by others.

We know moreover that the crime figures greatly underestimate the extent of domestic violence, as it is the most under-reported crime in our society, and even when it is reported, it frequently remains undocumented.[7] Further, reported violence rarely includes the many women who suffer emotional, psychological and financial violence. We also know that a great number of women kill themselves as a way of escaping from the violence. This is an area which requires immediate research.

A considerable amount of media and public attention in Victoria in recent years has been devoted to the Hoddle Street and Queen Street murders and other occurrences of violence inflicted by strangers, such as the abduction and murder of children. These have been accompanied by public outrage and concern to prevent such incidents from occurring in the future. While these homicides are horrific and the outrage appropriate, the focus on "stranger danger" has obscured the widespread nature of domestic violence in our society. There has been an absence of public and media outrage at the rate of domestic homicide, which accounts for the largest single category of homicides.

When a woman is killed or assaulted by her male partner or ex-partner, or a child is killed or assaulted by his or her father, apart from some notable recent exceptions, it often goes virtually unnoticed by the media and community. When it is reported, it is usually represented as an isolated aberration or personal tragedy, and not as the social crime it is, with social causes that need to be addressed by the community. It is also rare for the long history of physical and emotional violence which has usually preceded a domestic murder to be acknowledged or reported. This hides the context of the murder and obscures the power relationship between the murderer and his victim.

In contrast, the recent Victorian case of Daniel Valerio, who was murdered by his mother's de facto, was highlighted by the media as a case in which a range of professionals and others in the community were seen as complicit in the abuse which resulted in his death. The media outrage surrounding the murder trial possibly represents a shift in the media's reporting of domestic murders involving children; however, we have yet to see a similar reaction in the reporting of domestic violence and murder concerning adult women.

The types of explanations for domestic assaults and murders commonly adopted by the media, and used by the medical profession, counsellors, police and the legal system, maintain the status quo of a society in which women's and children's needs and safety are not addressed. These explanations not only condone and perpetuate men's violence, but also deflect attention from the existing gender and power relationships.

Firstly, the abuser or murderer is usually portrayed as not so much a perpetrator as a victim; the corollary to this is that the abused or murdered woman is portrayed less as a victim than as a woman who somehow provoked or is to blame for her assault or murder.

Secondly, domestic violence and domestic murders are often portrayed and dealt with as trivial, and as private affairs within the family — as is reflected in the remarkably low rate of police charges against men who assault their wives or girlfriends, compared with other offenders. When Vicki Cleary was being stabbed eighteen times by her ex-de facto, twelve people watched. During the inquest, on being questioned about their failure to intervene, witnesses echoed this view: "We thought it was just a domestic, so we didn't get involved".

Thirdly, there is a belief prevalent in Australian society that domestic violence and murder mainly happen to other types of people, with "other" often referring to migrants or working-class people. It is commonly but falsely believed that men of particular national and class groups are more likely to be violent to their partners and children. Culture and class are used as a way to absolve the individual abuser or murderer from responsibility for his actions, perpetuate racist stereotypes, and make other people feel safe and more distant from domestic violence and murder.

The women & children who were killed

✳

Women and children murdered by their partners and fathers have usually been subjected to years of violence by these men. The extreme end of this violence is murder.

Most of the women and some of the children in this book were subjected to serious physical assaults and sexual, financial and emotional abuse, with almost all of these forms of abuse happening at different times. For many of the women, emotional — or what many women describe as psychological — abuse was the most relentless and deeply damaging.

Families and friends we interviewed describe this abuse and what they and the women and children they knew thought about it. Their experiences leave no doubt that domestic murder is an aspect of domestic violence: these deaths were not so-called "crimes of passion"; each was the culmination of an ongoing campaign of control and terror.

Vicki Cleary

Vicki Cleary was killed in 1987 by her ex-de facto, Peter Raymond Keogh. Peter Keogh was found guilty of manslaughter. He was sentenced to eight years jail with a minimum of six years.

Keogh claimed he had been provoked because he could not persuade Vicki to resume their four-year de facto relation-

5

ship and because he believed she was using what he claimed was their car to see another man. She had left him some four months before her death.

Keogh stabbed Vicki repeatedly in the chest and abdomen. The coroner gave the following description of Vicki's death:

> On the morning of Wednesday 26.8.87, Vicki left her home and drove in her motor vehicle to the place of her employment at ——. She arrived at work at about 8.10 a.m. and was straightaway approached by Peter Raymond Keogh who stabbed her a number of times to the face and chest region.

The police report of death states that Vicki was "found lying in [the] gutter..." and the court transcript states:

> Keogh had left home early that morning [the morning of Vicki's death] travelling by taxi to —— Road where he alighted and walked to —— Street. Keogh had earlier put on a pair of yellow overalls, a peaked cap, a bluey jacket and had armed himself with a pair of side cutters, a Stanley knife, a pair of surgical gloves and a sharp hunting-type knife. Keogh placed the knife in the leg pocket of his overalls but found that the sharp knife dug into his leg. He then made a scabbard out of cardboard to protect his leg.
>
> Witnesses state that when Vicki's vehicle pulled up he walked straight across the road towards the car. It is not clear what ensued but the victim was seen being attacked in the open front passenger doorway of her Ford motor car. Witnesses observed Vicki struggling with Keogh who was seen to strangle her and place his hand over her mouth while he stabbed her repeatedly. The victim's screams were heard by many witnesses in [the] street and at the conclusion of the assault Keogh was seen to casually walk across to the opposite footpath and walk towards —— Road.
>
> Keogh then made his way across to an auction room which backs onto —— Street, where he met up with an

acquaintance, [who] noticed Keogh was a bit "toey". They drank coffee together and discussed the upcoming auction of furniture.

Vicki died two hours after the stabbing. Her mother, Lorna, was disappointed that there was no opportunity at the trial to describe the events that led up to Vicki's death. She was particularly frustrated by the fact that others could talk about the relationship between Keogh and her daughter, yet she was never asked to repeat what Vicki had told her. At the trial a witness had said he thought the relationship was a loving one. Lorna said, "this was far from the truth. Although we were a close family I was not aware of Keogh's threatening behaviour until after Vicki left him".

Family/friends quoted: LORNA (mother), DONNA, ELIZABETH (sisters), PHILIP (brother).

Ann Dyson

Ann, thirty-four, was strangled to death by her husband of thirteen years, Mick Dyson, two years after she had separated from him and two days before their divorce proceedings were to begin. Dyson's plea of self-defence was successful and he was acquitted of all charges without having to say a word. During the trial he admitted strangling Ann but said he had acted in self-defence after she attacked him with a knife. The Crown alleged Dyson had not acted in self-defence and had intended to cause serious injury to his wife.

During her marriage Ann was subjected to physical, financial, sexual and emotional abuse by her husband. Her family reported that things went wrong early in the marriage. "He was moody, sour, never consulted her or told her things, liked things his own way; it was mental torture…She lost her confidence. He was always at her."

According to a neighbour, "She just couldn't please him. He wanted a spotless house and expected her to be pencil slim all the time". A member of Ann's family said, "What she was saying really, was that Mick used to play mind games with her, he was always putting her down and she would do anything and everything that Mick asked of her to try to build herself up in his opinion". A witness at the trial said, "Mick was insanely jealous of her, he would not let her out of the house".

A relative told us, "We had family gatherings and Mick would always be vindictive to Ann. She would walk and he would trip her over, and if she would cook something at dinner parties — she'd spend all day cooking it — he would tell her how terrible it was and how he wouldn't eat any, just throw it aside".

A family member said, "She thought it was her. She went to a psychiatrist. She said she had lost all inside her and didn't feel she was worthwhile any more. She felt she was ugly and that she was nothing. He had destroyed all that". The psychiatrist told her it was not her fault.

A friend said, "He used to put Ann down a lot, and hurt her sexually". Someone else said, "He demanded sex from her to the state where she was vomiting".

After Ann left, she was frightened. She told Dyson he couldn't come around without someone else there. But three months before he killed her, he broke the door down and physically assaulted her. After this she told a friend that "he had a look in his eyes as if he could kill me". He also threatened to take the children away from her. "He got out the front of the door, and he was calling her a slut, a bitch; all bad names, out the front — that's when he bashed the door down and they had an argument and Ann had bruises all over her and a cut on her lips." During this time Ann was living in poverty; Mick was well off.

Family/friends quoted: MARY (sister), other friends and relatives who did not wish to be named.

Margaret Riley

Margaret was thirty-three when she was beaten to death in the bath by her husband, Stuart Thomas Riley, in 1959. After the beating, thinking his wife was unconscious, Riley put her to bed, only to find her dead in the morning. Margaret's daughter, Jeanette, says he was believed to have panicked, wrapped his wife's body in cloth, dumped it in the boot of his taxi and driven around Melbourne. On advice from relatives Riley returned the body to the bed and then contacted the police. A post-mortem revealed that Margaret suffered an enormous loss of blood, a broken neck, fractured skull and internal injuries.

In the first trial, the jury failed to reach a verdict on the murder charge. At his retrial Stuart Riley was found guilty of manslaughter. The conviction of manslaughter rather than murder was based on the proposition that Margaret provoked her own death through her alcoholism. Initially he was sentenced to ten years; this was later reduced to seven years on appeal.

Margaret was subjected to physical, financial, psychological and emotional abuse by her husband, including frequent severe beatings, for many years. On one occasion he broke her jaw and on another threw her out of a speeding car. Police intervened on numerous occasions — because he was breaching the peace by being drunk, not because of his violence.

He would control Margaret's access to money to the point where she had to ask for credit at the local shop when she needed something. Their three children were frequently beaten by him and interrogated about their mother's behaviour. For example, he would quiz them as to whether Margaret had fed them and beat her if they gave conflicting replies. "One minute, the family would be sitting at the table eating," Margaret's daughter Jeanette recalls,

> the next minute, the table would be up-ended and the meal spattered all over the floor. There were rules, but there was no use trying to abide by them because they were subject to change without notice...I came home from school one day

and my mother was sitting on the bed with a towel wrapped
around her head, saturated with blood. She said she had hit
her head, but I found out later that he had tried to drown her
in the bath. He'd also broken her jaw.

Margaret's husband totally isolated her and the children
from family and friends and constantly criticised the children.
Jeanette says, "As children we lived in isolation and terror of
our father".

Margaret attempted to leave her violent husband many
times but had to return. There were no refuges, social security
pension or benefit for sole parents in the fifties.

Family/friends quoted: JEANETTE (daughter).

Laurell Anne

Laurell Anne was twelve years old when she was shot in the head
by her father Dennis Michael McBride, a former New South
Wales policeman, in 1988. Laurell died of massive head injuries.
A senior constable gave evidence at the trial that he "approached
the passenger's side door and saw McBride raise the gun, grab the
back of his daughter's neck and place the barrel of the shotgun to
her head". At the time McBride had with him in the car a .22
rifle and a shotgun, as well as the single-barrel pump-action shotgun with which he murdered Laurell.

McBride was found guilty of the murder of his daughter,
and was initially sentenced to fourteen years jail. His sentence
was later increased to eighteen years. The appeal court also
increased the minimum jail term given to McBride from eleven
years to fourteen years.

Laurell, her mother Kay and her brother Michael were all
subjected to physical and emotional abuse by Dennis McBride
over many years. Kay described one occasion: "He had assaulted
me badly after keeping me tied up in a caravan for four days.

He caused injuries to me which put me in hospital for two weeks".

During the marriage he threatened to kill Kay and the children. One time, according to Kay,

> He grabbed me and ran the blade of the knife around the front of my neck and then the back of my neck. As he was doing this he was saying he was going to kill me. He ran the knife around my throat but not heavily enough to cut it. He then said to me that he wasn't going to kill me but would go upstairs and get Michael and Laurell and cut their throats in front of me and let me live to suffer knowing that I had caused it.

Kay left her husband in late 1987 and the children stayed with Dennis until Kay could find a home for them and herself.

After their separation McBride told Kay that if she sought police assistance to return the children to her custody, he would "kill everybody". At this point he had the children and was keeping them prisoner in his home. Kay said, "He'd lock them in when he went out and keep the phones disconnected unless he was using them". A month after the separation Kay was able to rescue the children from the house where Dennis was keeping them.

Kay, Laurell and Michael met with McBride on one more occasion to discuss access and custody. At this meeting, he kept them all captive and subjected them to threats and violence for many hours. At one stage Dennis held a gun to Michael's face and pulled the trigger. Michael later told the Coroner's Court, "I was so scared…then he pulled the trigger. There was a silence just before it then I heard the gun go click. I looked up and saw a grin on his face".

After some hours, Dennis eventually agreed to them going together to get some dinner. On the way he dropped Kay and Michael off near their house, keeping Laurell with him. In his sentencing remarks the judge said, on the day of the killing McBride had become uncontrollably enraged and threatened his wife and his son with a shotgun. To pacify him, McBride's wife had agreed that Laurell could live with her father. After McBride left, his wife telephoned the police, who chased McBride's vehicle at speeds of up to 160 kilometres per hour. McBride had raised the shotgun towards a policeman who approached him, then shot Laurell in the head killing her instantly".

Family/friends quoted: KAY (mother), MICHAEL (brother).

Teresa

Teresa, thirty-two, was murdered by her husband, Mario, in 1988. She died in a rest area on a highway, where she was shot in front of her three daughters; Natalie, seven, Josie, twelve, and Chessy, thirteen. "We all tried to hide in the car as our Mother told us everything she owned was ours, then he shot her again and she died", said Chessy, who then ran back to the rest area, bleeding and screaming, as cars screeched to a halt. Shotgun pellets had passed through Teresa's hand and then scraped Chessy's face and chest, and hit her hand. Teresa died from internal and external haemorrhaging due to a shotgun wound to the chest. After murdering Teresa, Mario shot and killed himself.

The Coroner's report describes the murder as follows:

> Mario then alighted from his vehicle carrying a shotgun and approached Teresa's vehicle. After a short conversation with his wife he placed a shotgun through the open window of his wife's car then fired one shot from a twelve-gauge Belgium "L.P.G." double barrel-hammer shotgun. The three children then ran from their mother's vehicle. Mario then fired a second shot at his wife. Both shots hit the deceased, Teresa, fatally wounding her.

Teresa had been subjected to physical and emotional abuse by her husband; her family say that he was increasingly violent in the last two to three years of their fifteen-year marriage.

Her sister told us, "He'd shove her sometimes but it was mainly emotional and psychological threats". On a number of occasions he threatened to kill Teresa if she did not do as she was told; he also threatened her with a shotgun three or four times. Among many forms of emotional abuse, he prevented her from seeing a number of her friends and attempted to stop her from having contact with her family.

One of her children told the court: "My mum and dad have been arguing nearly all this year and my dad always starts it and blames it on Mum, because he thinks that she starts it always. Dad won't let Mum have any friends or let her go anywhere without him".

He was physically abusive to the children, who were also present when Teresa was being abused. One of the children told the court: "Dad has threatened Mum with his rifle before, it was last year sometime…He has hit Mum before, several times with his hands, then he makes up with her, so she wouldn't go to hospital…Daddy used to try and strangle Mummy and he would point his shotgun at us when he became angry".

Mario's mother lived with her son and family. She described her son's violence towards Teresa: "On about three occasions over the last year, Mario threatened Teresa that if she did not do as he told her, he would kill her. On two occasions he actually threatened her with a shotgun".

Family/friends quoted: ANNE (sister).

Jill Bayne

Jill was thirty-five when she was murdered by her husband, Keith Bayne, in 1983. They had been married for eighteen years, and he shot her dead six weeks after she left him. Jill had one son, who was seventeen at the time of his mother's death. Keith

Bayne was convicted of murder and sentenced to life imprisonment.

On the day of Jill's murder, Keith packed his son's suitcases and threw them out of the house. He then rang Jill at work, said that their son had run away and asked her to come and help find him. Jill spent her lunch break driving around looking for her son, and arranged to meet Keith after work to talk about him. When she arrived, Keith gave her a letter that he had written and while she was reading it he went into his bedroom, got out one of his five rifles, and shot her. The first bullet went through her wrist, then she fell to the floor. A friend of Jill's was told that he put his foot on her head and fired one bullet behind her left ear, then one bullet into each eye and two more into her head.

Jill was subjected to emotional abuse by her husband for most of her marriage. Her sister told us that there was a short period early in the marriage when he was physically violent. Jill left him, obtained custody of the child and moved in with her own family. But his continual harassment of Jill and her family caused so much trouble that she agreed to live with him again.

He would not allow her to get a job even though they needed the money, and prevented her going to a craft class. When she eventually did get a job despite his opposition, he was extremely angry. She wanted another child but he wouldn't let her and stood over her at night to make sure she took the pill.

He would not allow her to spend time with other people. Her sister described one occasion when she and Jill visited another sister:

> I talked her into it, and she came with me. We stayed for too long and I got lost driving back...When she tried to open the front door with her key it wouldn't work. Keith had put the deadlock on. So we knocked on the door. Keith opened it and said, "The shit gets delivered through the back door" and slammed the door in our faces.

Family/friends quoted: JUDY (sister).

14

Paul and Lisa

Paul, eight, and Lisa, five, were murdered on an overnight access visit by their father, Simon, in 1989. Their mother, Chris, said:

> I saw my brother walking across the park with the police. I was
> there to pick up the children. They told me there had been a
> fire at the house…and would I come with them. I went to a
> neighbour's house and I was told my children had been killed
> by Simon and he had set fire to the house, stabbed himself and
> told the neighbours that the children were already dead.

Simon was convicted of murder, sentenced to eighteen years jail and was ordered to serve a minimum of twelve and a half years.

Chris and Simon had been married for nearly ten years when Chris left Simon. He murdered their children and burnt the house down twelve weeks later, Chris believes, so that she would be left with nothing. The children were repeatedly stabbed, their skulls smashed and then burnt. It was reported that "he bashed them over the head and then stabbed them repeatedly with a steel rod he had fashioned into a lethal point. He then poured petrol around the house and set fire to it…he had spent weeks making a special knife for the job".

Chris told us, "It was established that the kids were killed about one p.m. A neighbour smelled petrol but dismissed it. They were found wearing their shoes. They would not sleep in the middle of the day. The fact that Paul [who was deaf] was killed first — Lisa would have heard what was going on. Part of the evidence was that Lisa had her shirt stuffed down her throat".

Paul and Lisa were physically and emotionally abused for many years by their father. Chris, too, was subjected to his physical, sexual and emotional abuse.

"He had such self-control", Chris told us. "If I said something out of line, I'd see the violence in his eyes. He was physically violent three times in the marriage. After the third time, I said I would not stay in the marriage if it happened again. After that he stopped the physical violence, but you could feel it. You could cut the air. I was terrified of this controlled reaction."

Chris also described how Simon demanded she stay up until he got home after midnight each night so that she was available for sex. "It didn't matter to him whether I wanted to have sex or not", but she often put up with this abuse out of fear. "Quite often I would have sex with him against my will to bring him out of these moods. It was like dealing with a very dangerous, spoilt child who had to have his own way all the time."

Simon didn't like her socialising with her family or other people, or going to the children's play groups. He would continually criticise her; she felt she could never express an opinion, and always had to say "the things he wanted to hear". She had to beg forgiveness for upsetting him, even though sometimes she had no idea what she had done. She made excuses and allowances for his behaviour and tried to bring him out of his moods. "This would drain me emotionally and physically as it often took many hours to do." Chris says that she felt angry inside, but there was no way of expressing that anger without running the risk of being bashed. She told us about the physical violence toward the children:

> Paul copped a lot of his violence. Because of his deafness he didn't have any communication skills. Simon kept a piece of rubber hose to hit Paul with. As soon as I hid it he would just get another one. At times I would physically come between them and one time he beat me for doing so. I felt I'd developed skills to calm him down but I couldn't help Paul all the time. Lisa was like me, she learnt how to talk him out of violence.
>
> …Finally after I had been threatened with guns I realised that I could not cope with the situation on my own any more and I called the police who advised me to take out an intervention order which I did the next day. It took five police to hold him down that night.

Family/friends quoted: CHRIS.

16

Christine Boyce

Christine Boyce was killed by her husband, Kevin Crowe, in 1987 when she was twenty-eight years old. Crowe was convicted of manslaughter and sentenced to six years jail with a minimum of four and a half years.

Christine's family told us that in the two weeks prior to her death she had lived in five different locations, knowing that she was in extreme danger. When she applied for custody of her children the Family Court ordered that she establish a home and that her husband be allowed access before the hearing.

On the day she was killed, Kevin Crowe came to her house for an access visit. She left him there with the children while she went out to visit her lawyer. On her return he shot her at close range with a .22 rifle, in front of her two daughters. She died almost instantly of shotgun wounds to her face and breasts — she was deliberately disfigured. It transpired that Crowe had hunted her down for two weeks with a loaded shotgun in the boot of his car.

Carmel gave us the following description of her sister's life with Kevin Crowe:

> Christine lived only twenty-eight short years — the last three a mixture of terror and abuse. Physical and emotional abuse commenced soon after she began living with him. Dinners would be thrown in her face, her artwork broken, her ideas abused, her daughters beaten, her friends made unwelcome, her childcare arrangements messed up and her family scorned. She was taken to live in a community with no support services and no public transport. She didn't have a car and didn't drive. He ensured her financial dependence by borrowing heavily for a house, car, truck and business, narrowing her options to leave. Then she became pregnant. She hoped that he would treat her other children better if he had a child of his own.
>
> My sister left on many occasions and always returned. She was dependent on the income from the family business

to pay for her home, truck, car, childcare, food etc. All debts were in her name. When the business went bad he left on one occasion, leaving her with a baby and a small child. The debts of the business and repayments involved in the truck, car and home quickly became overwhelming. Part of the economic abuse that she suffered was having to get an additional well-paid out of hours job to support the business, work in it, feed her family and service her debts. At the time he wouldn't settle the property so that she could settle the debts. He knew it was impossible for her. She became an escort to feed her family.

He returned to Victoria debt free, and moved back in with her holding a shotgun to her head, and blackmailed her over the work she did. She could not refuse. He insisted she keep working then used her work to justify her murder. He had ensured that she had entered into financial transactions that she never normally would have. She had previously no need for a truck and a car and had always lived in a rented house. She was personally frugal.

He knew that she had been unable to get social security benefits and that she had worked as an escort to keep her two children and pay off their joint debts. He had blackmailed her to ensure her total subservience. She still left after beatings although he would always find her. Finally she left for good. She feared his onset of moodiness and tried to get him psychiatric assistance. He threatened to take her children. She left fearing for the safety of herself and her children.

Before her death my sister had the courage to leave. In leaving she told people her living horror story. That she had the courage to tell it and that he no longer had any power in that relationship became her death sentence.

Family/friends quoted: CARMEL (sister).

18

Sue Murphy

Sue was stabbed to death by her husband Richard in 1987. She was forty-five years old, had been married for twenty-eight years and had two children. She was murdered nine months after leaving her husband.

On the evening he killed her, Richard was waiting for Sue in the car park near one of her children's schools. Sue usually checked for any sign of him in her rear vision mirror before getting out of the car, but this morning she didn't. She became aware of her husband only when she saw him approaching her side of the car. She locked the door immediately, but he started to smash in the window. A teacher ran away screaming to get help, but before it came Sue had been stabbed as many as fourteen times. She died on the way to hospital. It appears that he sat in his car and listened to the radio until he heard that she was dead, then killed himself.

He also appears to have made plans in case Sue lived. The house that they had shared, which Sue had furnished and maintained, had been smashed and doused with petrol except for the room he had used. Sue had been applying for divorce and a property settlement.

Sue was physically and emotionally abused by her husband throughout her marriage. Sue's family told us that she was subjected to "ongoing domestic violence, particularly psychological torture" including the destruction of her most loved possessions, and deliberate cruelty to her cat. He wouldn't let her have a social life; didn't like her having visitors or ringing her friends. She was never allowed to go out, except to work and even then she was not allowed to work overtime or on Saturdays.

He was effective in isolating her from her family. Although he was careful not to demonstrate his violence in front of them, rather keeping it private within the home, one family member said, "The family only ever stayed over once. We had to watch what we said in front of Richard because we knew she would cop it afterwards". Sometimes Sue pleaded with her family not to come over.

Sue rarely confided in anyone — she took seriously his threat to hurt anyone she did tell — but she once admitted to her mother that she was very scared of him. Sue's mother told us, "She was very scared, even to go to sleep…She never provoked him. She was frightened of him all the time. He never let her be". He also gave her little money for the house and children although he expected her to cover everything.

Just before Sue left Richard, he punched her and held a knife to her throat, tormenting her with threats; after she left he made her life hell. He tampered with her car, tore parts of her fence down and, after obtaining her silent number through a friend at Telecom, harassed and abused her at all hours. By obtaining and copying her keys, he got into her house and attempted to strangle her. He attempted to get the sympathy of her family to get her to go back. When her family stood by her he resorted to ringing and threatening them.

Family/friends quoted: ANNA (friend), relatives who didn't wish to be named.

Mirela

Mirela was thirty-nine when she was killed by her husband, Erol, in 1989. She was bludgeoned to death in front of her two children, aged fifteen and eleven, with at least eighteen blows to the head from a metre-long home-made chisel. One of his workmates gave evidence that Erol shaped the metal bar from scrap the day before he killed her. Erol pleaded guilty to manslaughter on the grounds of insanity, and is being held at the Governor's pleasure.

Mirela had been subjected to years of abuse by her husband. We do not know much of this history. Her friend, Helen, told us that she had only told a few people. "Since her death the children began to speak out about the long history of violence that neither she nor the children had spoken about."

She told Helen about a year before her death that her husband had a knife and she was quite frightened and had hidden the knife. Mirela also said that he sometimes perused gun catalogues. Some indication of her fear is conveyed in a dream she told Helen about:

> Mirela dreamed once that she was being chased, and when she turned around it was her husband. She had a sense of her own doom. She indeed often had strong religious dreams symbolic of her own death. But she always felt that she was strong enough to take it all upon herself.

Her mother believes that he planned to kill Mirela after she started talking about leaving. She said in evidence that she believed her son-in-law "planned for a year how he was going to take her life" and that she "believed he went to hospital a year earlier to try and make out he was mad to cover up the murder".

Family/friends quoted: HELEN (friend).

Gene Boncodin

Generosa Boncodin was thirty-four when her ex-husband, Charles Schembri, strangled her to death. She died in July 1989, five years after her divorce from Schembri. Her daughter Alice was six years old at the time of the killing; Schembri had had custody of her since the separation, having threatened to kill them both if Gene took Alice with her. Gene was killed when she arrived at Schembri's invitation to collect her daughter for an access visit. Schembri told police, "I just grabbed her around the throat and before I knew it she was on the floor…I grabbed her with both hands. I just couldn't let her go". Gene obviously struggled for her life, leaving scratches on Schembri's neck. Schembri pleaded guilty to manslaughter. He argued provocation and was given an eight-year sentence with a minimum of five years.

Gene was subjected to physical and emotional abuse by her husband for the four years of their marriage. During their marriage Gene left him three times because of his physical, psychological and social violence. Gene's husband was verbally and physically violent in his efforts to control her behaviour. According to her sister-in-law, "Gene really tried to please him... He was very hard to please".

He particularly resented her independence and especially her desire to work where she wanted. He would not let her work any distance away from home and frequently humiliated her publicly. He was rude to her friends, and suspicious. If she did not anticipate his needs he would erupt into rages. On one occasion he was physically violent because she hadn't cooked for him.

He was extremely jealous throughout the marriage and up until the time he killed her. Each time she returned she hoped that he was going to change. At one stage he sent her newspaper clippings about the murder of another Filipina and expressed sympathy with the man who had done it.

Family/friends quoted: NONA and ROSA (friends).

CHAPTER ONE

Power & control through violence

✳

THE HISTORY

Men's violence towards women and children is not about anger, it is not an impulsive action of the moment — the murders we studied were not one-off aberrations but were preceded by years of prior violence. The violence involved a process of the men relentlessly wearing down their women partners. Central to the violence were psychological abuse, mind games, put downs and the destruction of self-esteem and identity. In the lives of all these women and children it was coupled with direct threats and physical violence.

Men's violence towards women and children is a considered exercise of power aimed at maintaining control over them. When a man who is violent towards his partner and children has his control over them challenged, he will often inflict more violence to "teach them a lesson", to remind them "who is boss" and to intimidate and force them into complying with his wishes. The ultimate expression of this desire to control is the act of murder. The men who killed the women and children in this book were acting consistent with the belief that they were entitled to own and violate these women and children.

"Whatever form the abuse takes, inequality is inherent in the structure of the relevant relationship. Women who are politically, socially and economically oppressed are battered by men who are, comparative to them, politically, socially and economically dominant."[1]

He stayed with her, guarding her from anyone that could help her…he felt and used power, control and terror. (CARMEL)

Some men previously viewed women as their property and I think that is where the abuse often starts. And it is just taken for granted. Because men believe when they marry and become man and wife the wife becomes the man's property. And his children as well. So he is free to abuse his property or treat them how he likes. (Interviewee, Office of Status of Women attitudes survey)[2]

If the jury represented society's attitudes, that meant women were nothing more than bloody commodities of violent men. (PHIL)

Their marriage was not a happy one but one that I would call fairly normal. By that I mean Keith had as much freedom as he liked but Jill did what she was told. (JUDY)

Sometimes I dared to question him. He would warn me not to try to behave like a man. Women, he said, belonged in the bed and in the kitchen and should not question what a man has to say. (CHRIS)

A woman can't have male friends, especially if they're married because it's seen as an affair. Husbands use that as a way to get out of the blame. If she got cards for her birthday from men at the factory he'd blame her. (ANNE)

A lot of men assume ownership of their partner's life. They don't know how to love or respect. All they know is how to control, oppress and demean. (JUDY)

My father used to put us in a children's home for months at a time as a way of trying to change her behaviour. (JEANETTE)

He wanted more children. He was annoyed with me for taking contraception. He liked the children when they were babies. But as soon as they developed their own personalities and began to extend themselves he didn't like them — he disliked the lack of control. (CHRIS)

He wanted to possess and own her. She never went out without him. (LORNA and DONNA)

She wasn't allowed to go out. Mario worked night shift. If she was half an hour late home from gym his mother would tell him and he'd get angry. He'd follow her to work in the mornings. His control got worse towards the end. (ANNE)

Keith would not allow Jill to find paid employment despite the fact that the mortgage payments were very high and there was more than one option for cheap childcare. The reason for this is that Keith wanted complete control over his wife's life. Paid employment means independence and Keith would prefer that Jill was completely dependent on him than have money coming in. (JUDY)

Richard was jealous of Sue's time with the children. At one stage he wanted Sue to go and live in the country without the children. All he wanted was her body because he rarely communicated with her. He wanted to control her totally. (Sue's friend)

If I can't have her, nobody else will. (Ann's killer, a year before he strangled her)

When the police asked him why he killed Jill, he said if he couldn't have her then nobody would. (JUDY)

When she left him, he lost control of her and because he couldn't deal with his loss of control, he killed her. She was his possession. (Gene's friend)

And then she tried to have her own life…Maybe she didn't know what she was doing. (Ann's killer, in accounting for his actions)

When he reached the car the rifle was pointed down at the ground. The window of my mother's car was open and my father was talking to her. He was really angry and he said, "You've got to go home. You have to stay inside the house and not see your parents any more. You're going to be all right because I'm going to control your life". (Teresa's daughter)

He told both Tanya and Mary on separate occasions that he would rather see her dead than with someone else. (A relative of Ann)

When Mick realised that he could no longer control Ann and that she was going to have her own life, he became obsessed with trying to control and dominate her, until he finally killed her. (Ann's friend)

As soon as Sue was married, I was never allowed to go to the house to visit. Her nurse friends were not even allowed to visit her. (Family member)

Some of us suffer as victims of it, some of us lose our lives because of it. My sister was a beautiful, caring woman, and she lost her life because she was trying to gain control over something that was rightfully hers and that was her life. (JUDY)

He gave her a letter he had written and got one of his rifles. The first bullet went through her wrist then she fell to the floor. He put his foot on her head and fired one bullet behind her left ear, then one bullet in each eye and two more in her head. (Friend of Jill)

He killed the kids to get back at me. (CHRIS)

26

Families and friends of these dead women and children commented that the way the murder occurred was not often evident in the court and media accounts of the murder. The image presented is one of a woman or child killed by one swift shot or blow, and dying painlessly — fitting perhaps the explanation of the accused of having "snapped", "lost control" or "killed for love".

All of the killings of women and children detailed in this book were cruel and torturous, most involving multiple shots, stabbings and beatings, humiliation and a prolonged death. Margaret's husband murdered her by repeated beatings inflicting eighty-nine wounds. Lisa and Paul had their skulls smashed and were repeatedly stabbed by their father, who had also stuffed a shirt down Lisa's throat. In a number of cases children saw or heard the murder of their mother.

CHILDREN

Children are victims of domestic violence in a number of ways. They may be physically, emotionally and/or sexually abused similarly to their mothers, and they may be murdered. They may be witnesses to the violence inflicted on their mothers, and caught up in trying to protect their mothers by running for help or lying when interrogated by their fathers about their mothers.[3]

Some of the children in this book were murdered by their fathers, partly to further abuse or torture their mother. The other children, whose mothers were murdered, were also abused by their fathers. Below we have presented some of the accounts of the violence they endured. Some mothers were subjected to numerous threats that the children would be harmed if they did not comply with their husband's demands for custody

After separation children are not necessarily safe, just as women are not. Access visits are particularly dangerous times for both children and their mothers. In some cases access contact is a time violent non-custodial fathers use to harass, threaten, abuse and sometimes murder their ex-partners or their children.

Violence done to children

Simon would not just smack Paul. He would use cricket stumps, sticks, belts and the worst thing was a piece of rubber hose on him. I would hide these objects or throw them away, but he would always find a replacement...If he could not find a weapon, he would kick Paul or pinch his skin so hard that most of the time Paul was bruised. (CHRIS)

I was crying because I was so scared. He told me to take my hands away from my face. I took my hands down to just below my chin. I could see that he had the gun barrel pointed towards my upper body. He was holding it with one hand. He said something to me but I can't remember what it was. I think he abused me a bit more then he pulled the trigger. There was a click. I looked up and saw a grin on his face. (MICHAEL)

He used to question us about whether we'd had dinner or not, and we'd lie to protect Mum and say we had, and we'd say something differently and he'd go and belt her...You sort of felt responsible — "if only I'd given the right answer" — when really he was just looking for an excuse...I think he often used to threaten to take us away — he often used to take my brother off. I mean we were terrified — if he said go to bed we went to bed. (JEANETTE)

Even from the age of two, Simon would stand over Paul with a stick when he was on the potty chair to force him to go to the toilet. He would hit him every time he tried to run away from the potty without having done anything. No wonder Paul was wetting his bed right up to the time he died. (CHRIS)

He held the gun to Laurell's head and shot her dead. (Coroner's Court transcript)

There was one family occasion where Mick deliberately tripped his son, pushed him over on the concrete and all his knees got scarred, saying, "this is how to make him tough". (MARY)

My sister used to get beltings for taking my brother's dummy from him when he was asleep. (JEANETTE)

Dennis had the children virtual prisoners in his home. He'd deadlock them in when he went out and always have the phones disconnected unless he was making a call out. (Coroner's Court transcript)

Daddy used to try and strangle Mummy and he would point his shotgun at us when he became angry. (Teresa's daughter)

Witnessing violence

Teresa would call Chessy to sneak out and call the police. It got so that when Chessy saw it she'd go anyhow without her mother telling her. (ANNE)

He beat her to death. The kids woke up. The daughter saw him and pushed past him to get help. He grabbed her and beat her, but she managed to escape. The son woke up and saw his father beating his mother across the head. The father then took the son for a whole day. (HELEN)

I came home from school one day and my mother was sitting on the bed with a towel wrapped around her head, saturated with blood. I found out later he had tried to drown her in the bath. (JEANETTE)

Abusing children to control and abuse women

He came around and told me to warm up his food that he had not eaten at work...He put the dog outside, went to the garage and brought back this high-powered rifle. I immediately went to run away out the front door. I had my car keys with me for a quick getaway, but he grabbed me and pushed me back on the couch. He said he was going to take our daughter Lisa to live with him. I wanted to agree with everything he was saying at this stage so I said that was okay but I needed to know where they were living and who would be picking her up from school and looking after her when he was at work. My mind was racing. I couldn't let him take Lisa but I couldn't disagree with him while he was in this mood. So I suggested a reconciliation which is what he wanted. I tried to talk him into a slow reconciliation but no, he wanted to have sex straight away. (CHRIS)

Paul and Lisa were murdered on an access visit. Chris told us, "He killed the kids to get back at me. This was a major factor which was overlooked by the judge". Chris says that although Simon was depicted in court as a devoted father, "he said there was no way he would pay for the kids. I think his argument was with me and not the children".

The night before, Paul had a restless night. He woke up the next morning at nine o'clock. He had an awful dream. When it was time to go to their father's they didn't really want to go. I didn't force them, but I certainly coaxed them...When I drove off I looked over my shoulder and saw the kids looking up at him with trusting eyes. I had an urge to say goodbye again...
I can't believe they are gone, I feel them constantly. (CHRIS)

There was a short period early in the marriage when physical violence occurred. After this, Jill left Keith and lived with her parents. However in her haste to get out, she left her baby with her parents-in-law. I remember that she would ring and make arrangements to visit her baby on weekends. (She was working during the week.) She had to take a tram and then a bus to get to them. She would arrive at the arranged time to find that no-one was home. She would sit on the doorstep for hours before returning home in tears and very depressed, because she hadn't seen her baby. This happened many times and her mental health was such that she was very close to having what the medical people call a mental breakdown. (JUDY)

He grabbed me and ran the blade around the front of my neck and then the back of my neck. As he was doing this he was saying that he was going to kill me. He ran the knife around my throat but not heavily enough to cut. He then said he wasn't going to kill me but would go upstairs and get Michael and Laurell and cut their throats in front of me and let me live to suffer knowing that I would have caused it…I agreed with him that I would not ring or talk to him any more and that I would leave the kids with him and get out of his life. I think that is why he let me go… I went to the police and sought advice about a restraining order against him but I was frightened to do anything about it for fear of my children's lives. (KAY)

After the murder – the consequences for the children

It is hard to describe the immense impact on a child of having their mother killed by their father. Everything in their life changes. On top of the devastation of their mother's killing, there are enormous practical consequences centred around where and with whom they will live, and which relatives and family friends they will continue to see. If there is no family to look after them they may become wards of the state.

They may also have to see their father in prison on access visits whether they wish to or not. Some families spoke about the enduring terror experienced by children who were required to visit the man who had killed their mother. Further, they could end up living with their father on his release from prison if he is successful in his application for custody. Carmel told us that Kevin Crowe "continued making applications for her custody and access to her for six years after he murdered my sister. Her daughter lived in terror of him until he was deported".

CHAPTER TWO

Permission to kill

✳

I'm still angry that nobody stepped in. I know that a lot of people knew what was going on, but nobody stepped in. (JEANETTE)

I think Mirela died because we colluded to help the death of this woman. What do you think? The longer we are silent about it, the longer it will take to change things for women. (HELEN)

Research commissioned by the Federal Government in 1987 found that one in five people surveyed admitted to believing that it is all right for a man to shove, kick or hit his female partner under at least one of the following circumstances:
  • she argues with or disobeys him
  • she fails to keep the house clean
  • she refuses to sleep with him
  • she sleeps with another man
  • she doesn't have the meals ready on time[1]
  One third of those surveyed said that domestic violence should be handled within the family. Two thirds said that a woman who was beaten could always leave the situation.[2] Findings such as this are an indication of the alarming prevalence within the community of attitudes and assumptions that provide justification — even approval — for the continued exercise of control and power, and the related abuse and murder of women and children by men.

In most cases of domestic murder, abuse has been perpetrated by the killer for a long time, and in one extensive study overseas it was found that women who were murdered had called the police an average of five times prior to their murder to report violence and seek protection.[3]

The failure of police and others in the community to intervene has more than just immediate effects. It perpetuates a culture in which men and women understand that violence within a relationship is not serious, that it is private and will not be dealt with in the same manner as other violence in the community. These responses also indicate clearly to the victim that she is alone. She is the one who will have to try to take responsibility for her own safety, even though women often lack the social supports and financial resources to leave a violent partner, and women who stay in the relationship are powerless to change behaviour which is the abuser's responsibility and decision.

The beliefs and attitudes we hold as a community support and construct the sort of society we live in. Racist, classist and sexist attitudes determine the types of social, political and economic structures our society maintains, but it is not a one-way process. In turn, these structures also inform our attitudes. For example, although the police and other professionals can be seen to be acting in keeping with prevalent viewpoints about men and women and violence, they are also fundamental in constructing and spreading these same attitudes amongst the public. They are not only reflecting attitudes, they are creating them, and in this way can be seen, through their frequent inaction, to be partly responsible for the continuing violence against women and children.

Similarly, when the work of government departments and service providers is based on policies that assume that women are or should be financial dependents of men, that women are the ones who should be responsible for the care of children, or that violent men need to be given counselling to "control their anger" rather than criminal sanctions, they are responsible for perpetuating a culture and a set of attitudes and practices which are oppressive to women, and which perpetuate men's violence and limit women's options.

COMMUNITY ATTITUDES

Men's violence towards women and children is supported and maintained by a range of attitudes and social structures. Women and men grow up with different influences that shape their notions of what is appropriate, acceptable and desirable behaviour; these in turn shape their behaviours and expectations. Cultural practices and assumptions that position women as the property of men, and as the ones responsible for keeping a relationship or family together and happy, still operate strongly.

Women frequently feel that they are responsible for what happens in the house and in the relationship, with the result that they do a vastly disproportionate amount of work to improve communication or establish intimacy in a relationship. Women feel responsible for their partner's well-being and worry that men will not be able to survive without them. The dominant ideology has it that women are good at being emotionally nurturing and caring and that this is their responsibility and a measure of their success in life. This means that a woman will often feel a failure if she acknowledges or tells others that her partner has been violent, and will experience guilt for leaving a violent partner.

Women often stay in a relationship despite violence and the knowledge that their lives are at risk because they, and the community, believe that it is best for the children or that a family should stay together no matter what. Many women have endured the violence because they thought — and were frequently told — such things as that a child needs two parents, or that their partners were only violent because they were stressed, unemployed, depressed, had a rough childhood and so on.

In this chapter we have looked at some commonly held attitudes and how they contribute to a culture in which women and children's lives are endangered by men. Common assumptions about domestic violence absolve men from responsibility for the violence they perpetrate, blame women, trivialise domestic violence and regard it as a "private" matter. We consider the attitudes and practices of doctors, counsellors, police, lawyers and court staff, and how they perpetuate those attitudes which contribute to women and children's lives being at risk from men.

I always made excuses for him

Ann's sister told us of one occasion when Ann went back to her husband a few years before he killed her: "Ann felt sorry for her husband and thought that the way he was stemmed from his childhood and so she would try to keep the peace".

Chris told us of one period when "I had resigned myself to believing I was stuck with it. I stayed for the children. I always made excuses for him. I was always looking for the good points". Mirela's husband was diagnosed as psychotic a year before he killed her. Mirela had thought of leaving him, but she felt "a strong commitment to him, and had promised his mother that she would look after him".

The numerous explanations offered by members of the community for why men are violent to their partners and children tend to have one element in common — they deflect blame and responsibility away from the abuser, and place it elsewhere. These explanations allow men not to take responsibility for their violence, discourage women from leaving a violent partner, and allow professionals to continue their inadequate and often inappropriate responses to reports or evidence of violence. Some of the more common ones include: the violence is conflict rather than really violence, the man was drunk/unemployed/overworked/stressed/unable to control his "anger"/feeling powerless/unable to communicate/working class/migrant/mad/the victim of a bad childhood/not really loved by his mother — and anyway, he was "provoked".

Many women feel sorry for their partners and believe that the violence is caused by these extraneous factors — including blaming themselves. All these assumptions locate the need for change elsewhere than the abuser's behaviour, frequently with the victim, with the result that violence continues.

It is obviously not the case that men are violent for these reasons alone. If this was the case just as many or even more women would be violent to their partners. Women are far more likely to experience abuse, particularly of a sexual kind, in their childhoods than men, they experience more psychological ill-health than men, and are just as likely to be working class, migrants and all the rest of the reasons frequently used to account for men's violence. The fact that the overwhelming majority of domestic violence and of domestic murders are committed by men needs to be explained instead in terms of power and control, and the inequitable distribution of social and economic resources between men and women.

It was her fault

It used to be my belief that a lot of women provoked violence in their husbands and I think a lot of people truly believe that. That is just not true. (CHRIS)

I used to think that when women were murdered like this, they were deserving somehow and it takes something like this to make you realise. (Sue's mother)

I remember feeling that people somehow blamed my mother, that somehow it was her fault, and that if she was different, things would have been better. (JEANETTE)

The court heard that Christine's work, [which was] a result of his economic and physical abuse of her and her children, was the cause, or justified her death. "Good women" do not work as escorts. Christine did, she mustn't have been a "good woman". She must have provoked her death. The court said she provoked her own death. She walked into the room where she was faced with a loaded shotgun at close range and brutally murdered. All she had done was left him with her children and hidden for two weeks from him. (CARMEL)

People, including violent men, police, social and community workers and legal professionals, often excuse violence by some-how blaming the victim. Subtle and not-so-subtle beliefs and attitudes inform their response: maybe her father was violent to her mother, so she has learnt how to be a victim, or she has had these sorts of relationships before so it must be something about her, or she somehow deserved the violence or she provoked it; she was a slut, a nag or hopeless with money. Such descriptions are almost exclusively applied to women and often they are directed towards women from non-English-speaking back-grounds and working- and welfare-class women.

Explanations for violence which blame women are based on stereotypes of what a woman should be and deflect atten-tion and responsibility from the abusers. The choices that they make to use violence as a strategy to maintain control over their partners become obscured by blaming the victims — a man's boss may nag, but the boss is rarely the target of his violence. Such excuses disguise the fact that men choose to be violent, irre-spective of their partner's behaviour. Women who seek safety in women's refuges often report that their partners behaved as though the woman could do nothing right — either she was dumb or smart or frigid or demanding or a bad mother or lazy or obsessive or ugly or provocatively dressed. When this type of emotional abuse and victim blaming is combined with strong views about women being responsible for the happiness and emotional well-being of their families, many women feel shame and embarrassment about being victims of violence, as though it were their own fault. The prevalence of these attitudes frequently means that women will keep silent about their partner's violence, or cover it up altogether. They try even harder to do the "right" thing in order to avoid abuse and make the abuser "happy".

Many of the women featured in this book told only a few people of the violence inflicted upon them, and often only after many years. When they did speak out, some were encouraged by others, including professionals, to change their own behaviour, as though this would somehow miraculously put an end to their partner's violence. In subtle and not-so-subtle ways, women are given the message that the quality of the relationship is their responsibility, and therefore the violence is somehow their responsibility too, and something they should strive to change.

Privatising, silencing and keeping it in the family

I never revealed anything about my husband or marriage problems to anyone, not even to my parents. I felt it was a reflection on myself as well as on him. (CHRIS)

She wanted her marriage and relationship to be a success. She thought that she should have been able to cope. She found it embarrassing to be the victim of abuse as she was she was such a strong, self-contained and in-control woman. (CARMEL)

When Mirela died, the children began to speak out about the long history of violence which neither she or the children spoke about. (HELEN)

When Gene's ex-husband sent her a newspaper clipping about a Filipina murdered by her husband, Gene told a friend who later told police: "I didn't want to encourage discussion on that matter with her. I didn't want to become involved with her problems of this type".

"Other people don't want to know", said Sue's friend Anna, "because if they knew then they may feel they should do something about it". As Jeanette pointed out, "My sister didn't tell her kids either but I thought they knew. That's the shame and the secrecy, the stuff like domestic violence is a private family problem. It is accepted that there will be fights between husbands and wives, and that people are going to lose their tempers. It's just amazing how much goes on that we don't know about".

Abusers, too, are keen to keep the violence in the family. To people outside they often portray themselves as "good blokes". Anna told us there were "no hints about Richard's behaviour. You would never have been able to have picked up that in Richard's behaviour". They control their image: Chris told us of how her husband made it clear that he didn't like her talking to others about their home life and "grilled her" about what she'd said.

This is one of the more common and dangerous assumptions, that domestic violence is a private matter which is not the concern of the wider community because what goes on in the family home is "between a man and his wife". The number of people who are willing to accept the use of violence against women and children when it occurs within the family is alarming. The survey of community attitudes undertaken in 1987 found that "more than a quarter of both men and women (twenty-eight per cent) said that they would ignore the situation or mind their own business if they found out that their neighbour beats up his wife". It also found that "a third of both men and women considered that domestic violence is a private matter to be handled within the family".[4] Many other studies indicate widespread lack of support and intervention by the community. Of the consequences, one researcher comments: "A view of family violence as private engenders both a reluctance to get involved and a perception of the assault as non-criminal".[5]

Just a domestic

*There were eyewitnesses who walked past Vicki, and ignored her
because they thought it was just a "domestic".
…Twelve people saw her being stabbed and ignored her pleas for
help. If they had intervened her death may have been prevented.
She ran fifteen metres and fell into the gutter. Two men came
along and were just looking at her.* (Lorna, Donna, Elizabeth)

*I heard two distinct screams. I then sort of heard a couple of knocks
or bumps coming from the flat…thought no more of what I had
heard. I then went on about my business in the kitchen.*
(Neighbour who heard Gene being killed)

*There was a gelati van parked along the highway and we drove up
to it, to the gelati van, and stopped behind it and asked the man
in the gelati van for help. She goes, "My husband has got a rifle in
his car and can you help me, I'm scared". The man in the gelati
van just looked at Mum and said, "I don't know, I can't do
anything".* (Teresa's daughter — Coroner's Court transcript)

*Everyone knew, the neighbours knew, the teachers knew but no-
one did anything about it.* (Jeanette)

*When Ann ran to a neighbour, who was a senior policeman, to tell
him, He's threatened to kill me, he did nothing other than get his
wife to make her a cup of tea, and tell Ann to get back to him if
anything else happened.* (Mary)

Violence to a partner in a relationship is often regarded as "just
a domestic", or a private "tiff" rather than the serious violence
it is. It is treated as something private that no-one wants to get
involved with, something that is the victim's responsibility to
do something about, or just a normal part of a relationship.
Research here and overseas estimates that violence occurs in
between one third and one quarter of relationships, and a man is
the abuser in more than ninety per cent of situations.[6]

PROFESSIONALS' ATTITUDES AND PRACTICES

National research conducted in 1988 into the "knowledge, feelings, attitudes and behaviours" of the Australian community towards domestic violence found that professionals very often had "firm beliefs that physical assault is so normal and inevitable as to be tolerable and acceptable".[7] This meant that they didn't respond or responded inappropriately. This and other research indicates a tendency for professionals to focus on a range of issues such as alcoholism, stress and psychiatric "illness". These problems become the primary focus for intervention and the abuse is seen as being caused by them — the violence is not placed in a social context.[8]

Not surprisingly, the research found that while the professionals appeared secure and satisfied with their practice, the victims were not. The report concludes that "Failure by professionals to intervene serves to perpetuate the problem; Experiences of victims (perhaps the real 'experts'), when they sought help from professionals, were ineffective intervention, no understanding of their fear and need for safety, reinforcement and perpetuation of the situation".[9] The research identified two consequences: "Men were assured that their conduct was not serious and was really all right. Men were excused from responsibility for their conduct".[10]

In many instances women only approach these professionals after a long history of being abused. Research and anecdotal evidence indicate that the response is far from satisfactory. Many studies have been conducted which create a picture of inappropriate, unhelpful and inadequate responses by significant numbers of professionals, contributing to the severe under-reporting of domestic violence, and further placing the lives of women and children at risk.[11]

Although professionals are acting in keeping with community attitudes to domestic violence, because of their professional status they are also fundamental in constructing and spreading these same attitudes amongst the public. By their often inappropriate behaviour, they perpetuate myths that blame

women and absolve men of responsibility for violence and trivialise and privatise violence against women and children.
Through their frequent inaction, professionals are partly responsible for the continuing violence against women.

The medical profession

*She was seeing a doctor who knew what was going on, about his
violence and threats and that he had a gun. She was given sleeping
tablets. The doctor knew about the threats and put them in contact
with a psychiatrist for him. They were even seeing a marriage
counsellor. Neither of these "professionals" told her how dangerous
it was for her.* (ANNE)

The 1988 national survey into domestic violence conducted for
the Office of the Status of Women looked at the attitudes and
behaviour of professionals in the medical area. They found that
hospital staff often don't inquire about even obvious marks or
bruising and that casualty services lack sensitivity to, and fail to
identify injuries resulting from, domestic violence cases.[12] A
woman who went to a refuge after being severely abused, physically and emotionally, by her partner for many years was not
questioned by the staff at the hospital at which she sought treatment about the source of her numerous injuries, which, over a
two-year period, included a broken collar bone, wrist, cheek
bone, arm and ribs.

Doctors who see women with injuries, distress, depression
or anxiety as a result of being abused by their partners all too
commonly respond with referrals to psychiatrists or counsellors, or by prescribing tranquillisers. These responses tend to
convey to women that the violence is not serious, that it is somehow the woman's fault, or that it is a psychological problem of
herself or her partner. By not addressing the violence, the doctor further puts at risk the safety of women and children.

A refuge worker told us of a woman who was raped every
day of her five-year marriage, and was taken by her husband to

a psychiatrist because she was planning to leave. The man told his story first, then the psychiatrist asked the woman for her experience. The psychiatrist's judgement was that the woman was delusional and paranoid, with a persecution complex. She was given a high dosage of tranquillising and anti-psychotic medication. The effects of this medication meant that she had to stay in a life-threatening and damaging situation for several more months, being raped every day.

Another woman in refuge had been subjected to severe physical, sexual and psychological abuse for more than twenty years. She was also taken by her husband to a psychiatrist, who diagnosed her anger and depression as resulting from a hormonal imbalance. Her legitimate emotional responses to abuse were invalidated in her own and her husband's eyes, and she felt that she could not trust her feelings, her plans to leave or her ability to relate to anybody else.

Christine attended a public hospital after she was beaten by her husband, and was advised to try counselling. Her partner attended one session. She returned to him, having left after the beating. Helen told us:

> The psychiatrists who were treating Erol were in my view grossly negligent. Neither Mirela or Erol were fluent English speakers, yet an interpreter was never called by the psychiatrists. They did not understand what options there were. All Mirela knew was that Erol didn't want to be institutionalised. What choice did she have really? She was frightened of him. He was frightened of institutions. She'd promised to his mother on her death bed that she would look after Erol who was her only child of eleven to survive the war. Mirela felt bound by this promise.

Because of their expert status, psychiatrists are not only enormously influential on the people who see them as patients, but can also be influential in court. Phil, Vicki's brother, questioned the so-called expertise of psychiatrists in his description of the trial: "Psychiatric evidence was presented as crucial in establishing his claim to depressive alcoholic illness. This was despite the psychiatrist's agreement that he could have killed during a 'psychogenic wipe-out' but equally that he could have conveniently forgotten to remember his actions".

Similarly, the expert evidence given in court in regard to Teresa's husband seemed to give professional credibility to his oppressive attitudes to her. Rather than seeing him as responsible and in control of his actions, the psychiatrist diagnosed him as having "pathological" jealousy, rather than a desire to control his wife.

Counsellors and social workers

We were both encouraged to look at our contributions to the build-up of violence — as though it was something that just grew, and as though it was my fault as well as his. It was like I had somehow caused it. He liked this, and used it to say that it was my fault, and not his, and that he couldn't be responsible for what happened between us. (Karen, refuge resident)

Counselling did not help Chris either: "No one believed the fear. The marriage counsellor didn't believe my fear of the gun. She felt that I was paranoid because of my fears of him. I didn't want to bad-mouth him or upset him. She couldn't work out why I was so afraid". Despite Chris's fears the same counsellor decided she and her husband should have joint counselling. "She felt that he was quite harmless and that it would be quite safe to have sessions together so I agreed."

At separation counselling Chris was "advised to be more blunt and not to pussyfoot around"; however Chris's "pussyfooting" was a deliberate tactic to placate her husband. This danger was also present in the earlier marriage counselling she and her husband attended. "It was probably the worst thing to have at that stage, because I was made to feel comfortable by the counsellor in opening up to reveal my real feelings. It was not what he wanted to hear. It would have made him feel even more angry towards me."

The 1988 national survey found that many victims and survivors have had negative experience of counsellors. Some have felt blamed by them, others have been sexually harassed by them. Many found that marriage guidance counsellors have quite punitive attitudes towards victims of violence.[13]

Women who have spent time in women's refuges have reported that marriage counselling was a negative experience, frequently only reinforcing and giving legitimacy to their partners' excuses for their violence. Counsellors tend to frame the violence as a "communication problem" between the couple, or as deriving directly from the man's childhood experiences or, if the focus is on the man's behaviour, his violence is interpreted as inability to "express his emotions" or "control his anger". In recent years, men who are violent to their partners have been referred to anger management groups which, according to reports from women whose husbands have attended these groups, does not stop them being violent.

This way of dealing with violent men obscures the fact that violence is used deliberately by men to gain or keep power and control. It constructs the problem as a purely psychological one, failing to take account of the benefits gained by the violent partner and ignoring the fact that women's and children's lives may be under threat. The result is often that the woman comes to believe that the man cannot control his behaviour, that he needs her support and nurturance to help him overcome his "problems", and that not to offer this would be selfish or harsh — even if her life is at risk.

Police

The response of the police to domestic violence is, as with other professionals, determined by what they believe to be the legitimate social, economic and sexual roles of women and men. This informs their daily work practice and has serious implications for the safety of women and children. The role of the police and the power they are given mean that their attitudes and views have a serious impact and authority. This point is examined in greater detail in chapters four and five.

Courts and lawyers

The big thing about family violence is that it is accepted. A man kills a woman and it's okay. It's like he won't have to say anything. He can lie, and we won't ask him anything. We won't try and prove he's a bad person — we'll try and prove she was, or that it was her fault, or at least that she deserved it. Our legal system is a joke. (MARY)

In the stories we looked at, the contact with the court system — the Family, Magistrates', Coroner's and Supreme Courts — came both before and after the murder, to deal not only with criminal matters but also custody, access, maintenance and property settlement. The legal system is far from a neutral arbitrator of law and order; rather it prescribes certain codes of behaviour as acceptable or unacceptable and dispenses justice according to these yardsticks.

Commenting on an American study assessing the performance of judges, senior Canadian judge Justice Bertha Wilson said recently:

> They have found overwhelming evidence that gender-biased myths, biases and stereotypes are deeply embedded in the attitudes of many male judges as well as in the law itself. They have concluded that particularly in the areas of tort law, criminal law and family law, gender differences have been a significant factor in judicial decision making. [14]

Given the composition of the legal profession and particularly the under-representation of women in the judiciary, this is hardly surprising.

The legal profession as a whole is often criticised as a bastion of privilege. But one in seven Victorian solicitors is a woman, and some city firms actually have female partners. Judges on the other hand, are almost all chosen from the upper eche-lons of the Bar, a male-dominated club which makes the world of solicitors look like an equal opportunity utopia.[15]

The impact that this gender bias and the resulting judi-cial partiality has on women and children is evidenced in the findings of the Victorian Real Rape Law Reform Coalition's 1991 sexual assault phone-in. The phone-in found that "Victims most often suffer the devastating consequences of sexual assault in silence, that they have no faith in the police, and legal processes, that the courts prefer to uphold sexist stereotypes which blame the victim of the sexual assault rather than judge the actions of the assailant".[16]

More recently the rape and domestic violence judgements of Justice Bollen and Judges Jones and Bland have highlighted the judiciary's reliance on stereotyped views of women's and men's role in society. Justice Bollen, a South Australian judge commenting on rape in marriage, "appeared to imply that a man was entitled to resort to rougher than usual handling of a wife reluctant to have sex".[17]

The rape victim of this crime made the following com-ments to the *Age:*

> I was not allowed into the court room for that [the judge's summing up]. I had to wait until after [the case] to be told what the judge said...I read it when I got a copy of the tran-script. I was really outraged. I found it disturbing to read. I felt that most of [Mr Justice Bollen's] comments were his own personal opinions and impressions and they didn't relate to anything about the facts of law.
>
> ...There is something I really want to say and don't know whether you're allowed to print it. I was always led to believe that the address to the jury gave the message that it was

acceptable and okay to bash the wife and that's why I feel the jury came back with a not guilty verdict.[18]

The 1988 national survey on domestic violence found that magistrates tend to hold conservative and traditional views about marriage and the family and that they tend to be ignorant of the effects of domestic violence "which inhibit agreement or satisfactory settlement" of family law matters. It also stated that Family Court judges, counsellors and registrars have little or no training in the effects of domestic violence on litigation and on the conciliation process.[19]

The research found that:

> The law does not seem to deal with domestic violence effectively. On the one hand there is a reluctance to place it in the criminal justice system, while the law defines assault as a crime; on the other the Family Court appears to pretend that it does not exist...
>
> Family Court counselling is often used as a panacea to the problem of domestic violence and with disregard for the victim's fear...
>
> The Family Court fails to recognise domestic violence as an issue when dealing with property, custody, access and maintenance.[20]

The families and friends we spoke to were as critical of the attitudes displayed by lawyers, registrars and judges as they frequently were of their legal ability or the laws they relied on. Courts and lawyers were seen to play on sexual stereotypes that were regarded by family and friends as degrading the woman involved. In one case the woman was summed up by a magistrate as "selfish, demanding, verbally aggressive and sexually active". The man who killed her was described as "likeable, a gentleman, and not prone to violence". Much of the trial concentrated on her characteristics. When, during the trial, she was described as "resistant to performing household duties", the Supreme Court judge inquired about the state of her house in the following way: "Was it more like four student kids in a flat, or was it more like a good housewife's flat?" Did this somehow justify and explain her killer's actions?

As is common in domestic homicide trials, in the trial of Ann's killer, much effort was expended by lawyers on trying to portray him as a nice, gentle, decent man, and Ann as a woman who was somehow to blame for her own killing. This included asking questions about her relationships with men subsequent to the separation.

The sections on the legal system in chapters four and five further detail the way these attitudes are translated into the legal processes.

CHAPTER THREE

Leaving

✳

WHY WOMEN STAY

"How am I going to cope with the kids? Where will I go? What will I do? Why can't he leave? I'm happy here", she'd say. "He'll find me wherever I go." (ANNE)

Women face many obstacles in leaving a violent partner, particularly if there are children. The attitudes of society and of the professionals from whom women seek help tend not to support them in their attempts to leave. There is a lack of secure and affordable housing and adequate income support for women escaping violence. Leaving often doesn't stop the violence, and may in fact exacerbate it — it is often after leaving that women and children are killed by their ex-partners and fathers. It is a failure of our society that the safety of women and children subject to violence is not given more priority.

Keeping the family together

She suffered a lot of guilt for going against the social expectation that a woman stays and cares for her family, no matter what. (JUDY)

You're brought up to keep the family together. (ANNE)

As we have seen, women tend to feel responsible for the happiness of their families and the health of their relationships. Even when they work outside the home, they usually carry the burden of household work and caring for children. The dominant ideology has it that a woman is good at being emotionally nurturing and caring, and that this is her responsibility and a measure of her success as a woman. This ideology, combined with the idea that a woman is somehow responsible for violence against her — that she deserves it or must have provoked it — means that many women feel a failure if they acknowledge or tell others that their partner has been violent, and many feel guilty for leaving a violent partner.

Some women stay with violent partners, knowing that they are in danger, because they believe they should try hard to make the relationship work. There is often a lot of pressure on women to keep the family together and give the man another chance. Many women stay in the hope that things will change, because they believe they should for the children's sake, or even out of sympathy — believing the excuses that their partners are only violent because they are stressed (or unemployed, depressed, have had an unhappy childhood and so on). Women who do leave violent partners or who depart from the role of wife and mother at home often suffer considerable guilt for rejecting powerful social pressures.

Mirela's friend Helen said, "She had started to talk about leaving with others and presumably with Erol as well. But she still felt a strong commitment to him, and had promised his mother that she would look after him".

Members of Ann's family now realise what a mistake it was to encourage her to reconcile with Mick "for the sake of the kids and because we felt sorry for him". Their attitude now is:

> When someone is saying things are not all right in the marriage, listen and don't just think the old wrong things like "a marriage should stay together" or "it's good for the kids". We are so upset that we didn't listen enough and that we fell for Mick's "poor me" sympathy plays, hook, line and sinker.

Teresa's sister said, "Women should be told not to under-estimate their partners. If he threatens you, believe it. Don't hang around".

After years of living with a violent partner many women lose their self-esteem and sense of identity. Ann, for example, thought she had to be "pencil slim" and went to a psychiatrist because she thought there was something wrong with her. The sense of shame and failure often felt by women in this situation and their frequent reluctance to discuss it with other people mean they don't get the necessary support and encouragement to leave. Some women's partners actively restrict their access to the outside world, for example by preventing them from gaining language skills that might enable them to seek assistance. For many women the constant abuse and threats to themselves, their children and other family members, mean that leaving is not possible. Lorna and Donna told us how when Vicki tried to move out, "he had the keys and had pulled at her hair and abused her. She told him that she was leaving on Saturday night. He raped her and tried to strangle her".

For non-English-speaking women, making a decision to leave a partner who is violent can involve leaving their entire community. This can mean that the woman is isolated from any-body who speaks her language or understands her culture. Further,the decision to leave exposes her to the racism of indi-viduals, agencies and institutions that she will be forced into contact with.

His violence continues

She put up with it for so many years. She was living on the edge. She'd had enough. (Sue's mother)

That day she must have just had enough. (Teresa's sister)

Despite all this, women do decide to leave even though they know it is dangerous. This is often seen by the violent man as a direct challenge to his power and control over her, and some men become more violent. A New South Wales homicide study found that forty-six per cent of women killed by their husbands had either left or were in the process of leaving their husbands when they were killed.[1]

Community workers and family members who have tried to help women and children leave violent men describe a range of strategies men have used to intimidate and harass their partners, and ultimately force them to return. Women have been rung hourly around the clock by callers who immediately hang up; they have had threats in the mail, their homes graffitied, their tyres slashed, their parents bashed, their children stolen from the school grounds, their mail interfered with, their friends harassed, their workmates given false information about them and a myriad of other forms of violence and intimidation. Ultimately, there is the threat, and all too frequently the reality, of murder for either the woman or her children or all of them.

In all the murders we have looked at, the women who were killed or whose children were killed had left or were about to leave. Many of the women who were murdered had left only months before their death; others were murdered years after as they were divorcing and settling custody and property — this was the case for Sue and Ann. Men who are violent frequently kill when women attempt to assert their rights over what men regard as their money, house, assets and children.

Sometimes it is also the property itself that comes under attack. Men have threatened to burn down the house if there is a chance the woman might get sole occupancy or her share of the property in a settlement. After separation women have come home to find their houses trashed, the doors bashed in, the furniture smashed and everything they value destroyed, from photos to pets. Sue's husband smashed up the contents of the house and doused everything with petrol to prevent her claiming anything in a property settlement; Ann was killed by her husband just after her solicitor had sent him property settlement papers.

"TO GET OUT OF A SITUATION YOU HAVE TO HAVE MONEY"

To get out of a situation you have to have money…you have doubts about whether you can support your children. It's all a risk. (ANNA)

I remember my mother tried to leave many times, but she would always have to go back. The problem was there was nowhere to go, with no money and three kids. She used to stay with friends, but that would only be possible for a couple of weeks. Then there'd be nowhere else to go because she had no family who could back her up, so she'd have to go back to him. She also tried live-in housekeeping but that wasn't any good either because she couldn't have us kids with her. (JEANETTE)

Without access to secure and affordable housing and an adequate income many women and children are unable to leave the men who are violent towards them. If they do leave they are forced into a life of poverty.

Women's inferior economic status and the lack of financial commitment from governments to economic justice for women, means that their access to an adequate income and secure housing is severely restricted. The main sources of financial support are inadequate and unreliable. The social security option actually increases dependency, restricts movement, removes self-determination and increases women's vulnerability to men's violence. Women wanting to leave a partner who is violent are often deterred from doing so because the options supposedly available to them are so discouraging.

It would be simplistic to argue that women's financial independence and access to affordable housing are the keys to

55

eradicating men's control over, and abuse of, women and children. Many women who have succeeded in gaining financial independence from violent partners and have obtained their own housing have also been murdered. Nevertheless, if they had had an adequate source of income and secure and affordable housing available to them, they would have had a greater range of options and more chance of staying alive.

Violence against women is the result of gender inequality, and one major strategy necessary to combat such violence is to reduce inequality and powerlessness by delivering economic justice to women. Currently, government housing and economic policies are grossly inadequate. As a consequence governments must bear a heavy responsibility for maintaining what is, for women and children experiencing male violence, a murderous status quo.

Money to live on

I was working part time. I could support the children if I had a roof over my head, but I couldn't afford rent. For a week I would go back to the house to collect things, but he then changed the locks. Despite the fact that I contributed to the house payments the most, he saw it as "his house". (CHRIS)

Many women don't leave because they don't know how they will survive financially as sole parents, particularly with their options limited by economic disadvantage. Overseas and Australian research indicates that custodial parents (primarily women) are financially worse off following separation. By comparison, the economic circumstances of non-custodial parents (primarily men) improve.[2] Many women considering leaving a partner who is violent are forced to make a choice between further violence or a life of poverty.

The connection between women's economic vulnerability and the abuse and murder of women has been pointed out by women for many years. In 1983, barrister and writer Jocelynne

Scutt put forward the view that part of the solution to the problem of spouse assault lies in examining and developing the capacity of the system to deliver economic justice to women as a way of eliminating gender inequality and, hence, the violence that accompanies it.[3]

Women's economic disadvantage arises from a variety of factors. Some of them are to do with women's place in society and their traditional role within the family, and some are to do with structural inequalities in the workplace.

His money

He buys whatever he wants, but he won't let Mum have anything.
(Teresa's daughter)

Men's violence towards women has also often taken the form of economic deprivation, further ensuring that a woman's chances of leaving are severely restricted. The control or withholding of money can be used to humiliate, denigrate and dominate women who have little or no independent income. Many male breadwinners regard their earnings as their own, to do with as they please, rather than as family or household income. Money for household expenses is controlled by and dependent on the goodwill of the partner.[4]

Women who have lived with men who are violent towards them talk about how they were demeaned by their partner's control over their access to money, having to ask for money to pay for food, clothing and other essentials, and to account for every penny they spent. Typically, they were then abused for not being good enough at budgeting on the inadequate money they received.

Through controlling their partner's access to money, violent men are able to control her mobility, her opportunity to socialise with friends and her ability to enrol in classes or pursue interests. Her sense of dignity is progressively diminished and her chances of seeking safety are severely restricted.

When women seek economic independence through paid employment they are often thwarted by their partner, or the money they make is taken from them for their partner's use. For example, although Richard disliked Sue working and felt she should be at home for him, he happily spent her earnings. Vicki Cleary's situation was similar. Her family told us:

> He left his job and depended on her earnings. He wanted to possess and own her. She never went out without him. While she worked, he would stay at home and watch television...He arranged his life the way he wanted...Vicki was paying for a lot in the house. He used her name to get money...Vicki would often sign blank cheques so Peter could buy furniture. The receipts were in his name even though Vicki paid for it.

Women's work

Women are still regarded as primary care-givers to children and responsible for the domestic sphere in general. While some women choose to work at home, either paid or unpaid, others choose or need to work outside the home. The limitations of being primarily responsible for children impose numerous restrictions so that many women do not feel able to enter the workforce, and those who do, commonly feel torn by competing demands: they usually bear the double responsibilities of home duties as well as their paid work and are generally confined to low paying, low status jobs.

In September 1989, 222,500 Australian women gave family considerations as the main reason for not actively seeking work. Of these, 73,600 cited lack of suitable child care and 102,000 cited their preference to look after their children themselves.[5] There is a chronic lack of affordable and suitable childcare available to women. This is particularly true for non-English-speaking women who may want language-specific or culturally sensitive childcare.

58

Women are disadvantaged financially if they stay at home and care for their children — they seldom have an independent income. Further, women are not paid for the work they do in the home, and they do considerably more unpaid work than men.[6] Because women's work in the home is unpaid and undervalued, it is difficult to establish women's right to compensation for labour which is actually crucial to the economy but has, until recently, been disregarded in accounts of economic activity. In 1990, the Australian Bureau of Statistics for the first time valued unpaid housework at $142 billion — sixty per cent of the Gross Domestic Product in Australia. However, current Australian practice is still based on the United Nations System of National Accounts.[7] In the current system, war production has value, child care does not. This valuation of work is clearly gender biased; it denies that women's labour in the home contributes to the economy and therefore should be paid. Such a denial ensures that many women already vulnerable to control by their male partners or fathers are forced into economic dependence.

Labour market disadvantage

This dependence is aggravated by the fact that women are structurally disadvantaged in the labour market. In examining the current status of women in the Victorian Labour Force, the Department of Labour's Women's Employment Branch reported that women can expect to:
- earn a lower income
- receive fewer employment benefits
- be less likely to have access to superannuation schemes
- have less formal accredited training
- have fewer opportunities for career progression
- experience higher unemployment rates than men seeking paid employment[8]

Women's wage earnings in 1989–90 were, on average, only sixty-one per cent of men's.[9] Comparisons of minimum award rates, award allowances, earnings across industries, earnings by occupations, over-award payments and benefits all show that women earn significantly less than men. An example of this is that men's work frequently includes allowances for strength, dirt and industry conditions, whereas women's work rarely attracts comparable payments for repetitive work, high concentration and physical dexterity. The majority of women are employed in low status positions with limited opportunity for career development.[10] More than half of all employed women are found in two occupational groups: clerks and salespeople, which includes personal service workers.[11]

Australia has one of the most sex-segregated workforces in the OECD group countries.[12] This segmentation is so rigid that the labour market is often referred to as a gender specific "dual" market. The "primary" market has stable employment, high levels of skill and wages, good prospects for individual advancement and largely male employees. The "secondary" market, in which women are disproportionately represented, is one of relatively low skills, high labour turnover, low wages and few prospects for advancement or cross-over into better "male" jobs.In fact, there is greater occupational segregation now than in 1911.[13]

Working-class women and women from non-English-speaking backgrounds are the most severely disadvantaged by current economic systems.[14] "Non-anglo women…are concentrated in low-status, low-paid and unskilled jobs in labour intensive industries and insecure industries in the manufacturing sector. Compared to all women, high proportions of women born in non-English-speaking countries are labourers (twenty-one per cent) and plant and machine operators and drivers (seventy-one per cent)."[15] In addition, "single women and women born in non-English-speaking countries, both have below-average earnings but above-average participation in full-year, full-time work."[16]

Social security

Many women who leave violent partners must rely on social security, usually the Supporting Parent's Benefit or Job Search Allowance, for their income. Young women who are homeless have to exist on the Young Homeless Allowance if they don't have children. All types of pensions and benefits provide an inadequate income. "For women whose main source of income was government pensions/benefits", the Australian Bureau of Statistics has found, "the average annual income was $6,000, less than half of that for all women".[17]

It is estimated that sixty-two per cent of sole parent families are living in poverty after paying rent: "Sole parent families are much more vulnerable than their two parent counterparts to poverty and the effects of income inequality. They are more likely than couple families to be in receipt of a pension or benefit and their poverty rate is over four times that for all families."[18]

This is particularly the case for those forced to rent privately, as most sole parent families and women escaping violence are. The Tenants' Union of Victoria points out that "a 1989 Ministry of Housing and Construction statement accompanying its 1989 report on rent prices indicated that a sole parent with one child receiving the Supporting Parent's Benefit would pay eighty per cent of their weekly income for the median two-bedroom rental housing."[19] The Ministry also reports that less than one per cent of private rental properties in Melbourne are affordable for sole parent families and pensioners.[20]

As well as living in poverty, women on social security are subject to policies that persist in treating women as dependants of male wage earners rather than as primary wage earners themselves. The financial hardship involved in depending on social security is exacerbated by the "poverty trap". For example, effective marginal tax on any earnings above the allowable limit for sole parents is an astronomical sixty-two per cent. This discourages employment and locks them into a cycle of dependence on benefits insufficient to keep them above the poverty line without resorting to fraud.

Case studies collected in 1990 by the Council for Single Mothers and their Children and the Welfare Rights Unit of Victoria highlight the problem. Discriminatory practices by the Department of Social Security (DSS) include excessive reviewing, abuse of discretionary powers, not following correct procedures, giving incorrect information and intimidating sole parents. A typical case study is as follows:

> Ms L, who has four children, received the Sole Parent's Pension. One Friday, a Department of Social Security field officer visited her and alleged that she had a man living with her. The DSS called her for an appointment at the office and asked her to sign a statement (no copy was given to her). She was subsequently told by the field officer that her boyfriend could only visit on weekends and not stay overnight. Ms L was also told that she could incur a $2,000 fine plus paying back an overpayment and possibly be imprisoned if the DSS found out a man was living with her. Ms L was intimidated by this process and decided to live with her boyfriend and cancel her Sole Parent's Pension. Ms L's boyfriend applied for the married rate of the Unemployment Benefit. Having gained economic control over her, he then became physically violent towards her...[21]

As this example demonstrates, the de facto rules are applied in a way that is intrusive, humiliating and designed to portray a woman as either dependent on any man she is involved with (whether she is in fact living with him or not), or else suspiciously and temporarily independent (and requiring vigilant policing). As a result, women are often forced into financial dependence on a man. This may be much cheaper for the state, but makes women more vulnerable to financial exploitation and other forms of abuse from their male partners. Ultimately these discriminatory practices increase financial hardship for women, and put their safety at risk.

Young women

Of great concern are the numbers of young women who are forced to leave home because of their father's, stepfather's or brother's violence. The Young Women's Housing Shopfront, a referral and information service in Melbourne operated by the Young Women's Housing Collective, handles thirty to forty enquiries each week, eighty to ninety per cent of which are from girls and young women who state that they had to leave home because of some form of physical, emotional or sexual abuse.[22]

Most young women do not have access to employment and the Young Homeless Allowance is totally inadequate, as are unemployment benefits (which are only available for those who are over eighteen). Thus, many young women who become homeless must find accommodation in squats or in short-term emergency accommodation, or exchange sex for accommodation, or sometimes end up in correctional institutions. There are housing programs available to young people, but very few that are single sex and certainly not enough to meet the demand.[23]

For young women, there is a chronic need for more gender-specific services which reflect the diversity of their needs and experiences. These services need to provide support and independence, they should not be services that are imposed on young women as a means of institutional control.

SOMEWHERE TO LIVE

Basically it never fails to enrage you when you think that all these women and children are seeking refuge. While overwhelmingly the men who offend and probably continue to offend are basically unaffected and *still living at home...* (Refuge worker)

There should be more refuges for women...and more telephone boxes and ways to call when you haven't got any money. There's nothing worse than being chucked out of your home and you're half dressed and bruised and you have no money. That's when you need instant help. (KAY)

Long-term housing options, such as home ownership, public housing or secure affordable private rental housing, are often difficult for women to gain access to. Women's refuges and emergency accommodation can offer some, but not all women, immediate escape from violence. They are unable to ensure that women have ongoing, secure and affordable accommodation.

Short-term accommodation

There need to be more refuges, and more housing that women can afford. Also, we need refuges that are tailored to women's needs. Say refuges for women who are of the Islamic faith, or refuges for only single women. Now, a woman doesn't get a choice; she just goes in to the refuge where there is room, or she doesn't get a place in a refuge. (ANDREA, a refuge worker)

Hilda got married when she was eighteen. Only two weeks after the wedding she told her mother that if she had anywhere to go she would leave him. But money was tight for her family and Hilda had none of her own, and in those days there were no refuges. She had to stay until these resources were available. She put up with the violence for twenty-six years. (Family member of a woman murdered by her husband in 1990)

According to the Women' Refuge Referral Service, this year eighty per cent of women who sought accommodation in a refuge could not be housed.[24] Statistics from other services are equally grim. The Fitzroy/Collingwood Accommodation Service, for example, only had three flats available to women and children in 1990, in Victoria's largest inner urban region. In the quarter to the end of December 1990, requests for accommodation were continuous, but only 116 placements were made.[25]

Accommodation is scarce because of funding shortages. Short-term accommodation services are forced to apply extensive eligibility criteria which exclude many people in need. One such criterion, applied by some services, is that women must have somewhere to go to after the accommodation time limit is up. Many accommodation services feel it is more traumatic and less useful to house women who are just going to be homeless again at the end of a few weeks. Women escaping domestic violence and in need of crisis accommodation, however, rarely have anywhere else to go.

Women searching for emergency accommodation usually end up in rooming houses which are inadequate, inappropriate and often unsafe. Women run the risk of being mugged, bashed, raped or harassed by men in the houses. Their small numbers make them visible and vulnerable (women make up only eighteen per cent of rooming house tenants) and there are very few rooming houses for women only.[26]

Women leaving violent partners need accommodation which is not only accessible, culturally relevant, supportive and affordable but also stable. Emergency accommodation is usually so short-term that it is completely unsuitable. Women's refuges offer shelter for up to three months. Emergency accommodation offers anything from overnight to a few weeks stay. Young women can be particularly affected, tending to move in and out of youth refuges, emergency accommodation and unstable shared accommodation, and on and off the street. The Victorian Council of Social Services noted in a 1990 report that this pattern is likely to get worse, partly because of the lack of government commitment to youth accommodation needs.[27]

The lack of diversity of options in short-term accommodation creates further discrimination for groups of women who are already marginalised. For example, there is a chronic lack of culturally sensitive support services, and of services which meet the specific needs of women who are alcohol and/or drug dependent or have psychiatric histories.

There needs to be more gender-specific accommodation that offers support to women who have particular needs such as psychiatric support, and there needs to be accommodation which caters for all cultures and ethnic groups. This would entail refuges and emergency accommodation services actively making themselves accessible to women from culturally diverse backgrounds through their employment practices and organisational policies, through the information they provide and through contact with relevant communities. There also needs to be accommodation which offers women secrecy of address. Currently the refuge program provides this and the State Government needs to make an unequivocal commitment to continuing this program as a means of ensuring women and children's safety at times of crisis.

Many emergency accommodation services are working under increased pressure to meet demand without an increase in funding. Consequently, there is overcrowding and under-staffing of accommodation services, which means they are forced to offer minimal personal and practical support to women suffering trauma as a result of violence.

Long-term housing

We have seen how difficult it is for women, especially those relying on social security, to afford private rental housing or home ownership. Women-headed households are under-represented among home owners and purchasers; they are more likely than men to be public housing tenants and to be renting on the private housing market.[28] Further, security of tenure for private rental is not guaranteed and women can be subject to harassment and pressure from real estate agents and landlords.[29]

Many women leaving partners who have been violent to them must rely on public housing as their only long-term accommodation option (twenty-four per cent of lone mothers live in public housing).[30] And yet demand for public housing in Australia far outstrips availability. In early 1990 in Victoria, there were 36,800 people on the waiting list.[31] Stock acquisition by the Ministry of Housing is minimal compared to demand. One researcher comments that "the Victorian Government has the worst performance of any State in Australia in terms of per capita spending on housing".[32] General housing funds have also decreased in real terms and continue to decline.[33] Thus women often have to wait long periods to gain access to public housing; minimum waiting times are around two years. Although women escaping domestic violence have priority, they must disclose the violence and substantiate that it has occurred. Even then, waiting periods of up to eight months still occur.[34] "The difficulties", according to a refuge worker,

> include first and foremost the lack of public housing. Even when a woman is not knocked back on a technicality or the unrealistic assumptions of the priority panel, priority is taking three to eight months. Ministry of Housing seem to be concerned more with keeping women off priority than anything else.

But even when women are able to obtain public housing, it is not always suitable. Women escaping violence are particularly disadvantaged: they are more likely to be allocated the least desirable housing because they are in crisis. A report by Women In Supportive Housing refers to the "punitive attitude" of the Ministry of Housing when it responds to women and children in crisis.[35] Refuge workers report that when they apply for priority housing there are long delays in getting appointments, delays in getting information, excessive demands for supporting documentation as evidence of domestic violence, misinformation and long delays in the allocation of a house after approval has been given by the Department of Housing.

Another problem identified by refuge workers is the lack of consistently applied criteria between Ministry of Housing regions, so that some women are granted priority while other women in equally drastic circumstances appear to be rejected on technicalities. A refuge worker gave the example of a resident who had been refused priority housing because the priority panel believed her case "wasn't urgent enough". "The woman is forty-five, speaks little English and has four children to support. She's been through a war in another country — now this…We see more and more cases like this."

Instead of making flexible and constructive interpretations of what is at times unclear policy, staff in some cases adopt rigid and unsympathetic stances, asserting, for example, that a woman in a refuge is "housed" and therefore not eligible for priority under the homelessness guidelines. Further, the department's definition of domestic violence does not include the assault of women who do not ordinarily live with their partners, nor does it include co-tenants or lesbian and gay couples. The conditions for eligibility require needless amounts of proof and documentation of violence. In many instances a woman has no "proof" — the police and other "experts" in the field may not have been aware of the violence and therefore cannot give supporting evidence. A woman in this situation, especially if she has not been able to obtain refuge, has no documentation and hence no case.

A further significant difficulty for women attempting to gain access to public housing is the eligibility requirement that arrears for previous public housing tenancy be paid. Often it is not the woman who has incurred the debt, but her violent partner. Women who have fled public housing due to violence and need a transfer to alternative public housing, or who are reapplying, must make a "satisfactory agreement" to repay any arrears. This usually entails payment of a lump sum of between $599 and $1000, as well as an ongoing five per cent of income until the arrears are paid. Few women in crisis have access to this kind of money. Women on low incomes and Koori women are particularly disadvantaged by the rent arrears policy of the department. Those Koori women who have taken part in rent strikes as protest against white invasion and the fact that white people have not paid the rent, are unable to get priority without enormous and unworkable forced-debt repayment.

Another problem with Ministry of Housing eligibility requirements is that women have to attempt to get private rental accommodation, using the Bond and Relocation Scheme, before priority will be considered. This means going to as many real estate agents as possible and getting signed forms as proof that there is no housing available which would cost less than fifty-six per cent of a woman's income. This requirement amounts to little more than an exercise in harassment since there is very little affordable housing available in the private rental market for sole parents. A sole parent with one child receiving the Supporting Parent's Benefit would pay eighty per cent of her income for an average two-bedroom rental; in addition, real estate agents discriminate against women with children who don't have a male partner. As one refuge worker put it, "Private rental is in no way easily accessible nor affordable. There is definite discrimination if a resident is unfortunate enough to let slip that she is in refuge".

For Koori people, gender-based discrimination is compounded by racial discrimination. Koori women report that the racist stereotyping of Koori people as drunken, dirty and noisy, added to stereotyping of and prejudices against single women with kids and no money, makes rental housing impossible to obtain.[36]

The Department of Planning and Development purchase, allocation and construction practices are historically inadequate. Women with dependent children can be housed on the outer fringes of suburbs, poorly serviced, cut off from social and traditional networks, with inadequate public transport and few employment opportunities. Language and cultural barriers create additional hardship for women from non-English-speaking backgrounds.

CHAPTER FOUR

Before the killing — the legal system

❋

For many of the women discussed in this book, their first encounter with the legal system and how it deals with domestic violence began when they sought police protection from the violence and the laying of criminal charges. As we will see, the legal system completely failed to protect them.

In this chapter we outline the ideology and culture of the police, what they can do when responding to violence in the home and — drawn from the experiences of the women and children documented in this book — what they are actually doing. The discrepancy between what they can do and what they are doing is discussed, and the attitudes which inform the behaviour of police described. We also look at the women's, children's and families' experiences of the court system in relation to the violence which preceded the deaths, and at the issues of access, custody and property settlement. We show that the legal system often fails women and children in its inadequate response.

POLICE IDEOLOGY AND CULTURE

I said to the police, "Does she have to be killed before you do anything?" Basically he said yes. I went back to the sergeant after she was killed and asked him, "So a bit late now?" He didn't say anything. (ANNE)

The police are often assumed to be neutral enforcers of a neutral legal system, which operates for the "good of society". The experience of women and children in the criminal justice system belies this. The police use the criminal law in a small minority of reported cases of domestic violence, even though the assaults are often severe and are frequently reported. If these assaults were perpetrated by strangers, the police would use the criminal law as a matter of course.

The definition of what crime is, however, is determined by the most powerful members of society. For example, the taking away of Aboriginal children from their families and communities by state authorities was and is experienced as kidnapping by those families and communities, but was and is defined by the state as a "protective social welfare initiative". Until recently taxation fraud was seen to be "bending the rules" but social security fraud has always been seen and punished as a crime.

Police culture — masculinist culture

The way police enforce the criminal law perpetuates an ideology, part of which is concerned with masculinist values. "Masculinist" refers to an ideology which privileges the interests of particular groups of men over women, as well as other groups of men. Although lip service is paid to the "protection of all individuals' rights", in practice this is not the case for many women and children.[1]

What emerges in the criminal justice system is a particular view of the role of women: "the criminal justice system is not designed to empower women but to maintain traditional family structures".[2] Culturally sanctioned views of women and women's roles are embodied in legal, economic and financial discrimination against women and are expressed through social institutions and processes, for example in the fields of health, welfare, education, science, the military and the police.[3]

An important example not only of the biased nature of criminal law enforcement but also of the inter-relationship between social structures and attitudes can be seen in the police's inadequate response to reports of assaults in the home. Many police appear to act on assumptions: that women are the property of men, women are somehow to blame for violence against them, men aren't really responsible for their violence against their partners, and that violence perpetrated by men on women is a trivial or private "tiff" rather than a criminal matter like any other assault.

In turn, the lack of action by the police serves to reinforce all the above attitudes and assumptions. The perpetrator of violence is given a clear message that he can do what he likes with "his" woman, that his behaviour isn't really criminal, that his behaviour is a "social" problem and not a criminal matter, and that the members of the community responsible for providing legal sanctions and protection will not interfere with his actions. This means men frequently see themselves as above the law and continue their violence as they wish, even to the extent of murdering their partners and children. Paula, a refuge resident recalled, "He knew that they would do nothing, because they never had before. He used to taunt me with the phone, saying, 'Go on, call them'. Then he'd laugh".

Inaction or inappropriate action by police gives a woman the message that the man can do what he likes, that her safety is not going to be the concern or responsibility of the police, possibly that the violence is only trivial, a social problem or somehow her fault, and that she, unlike someone assaulted by a stranger, is not going to be accorded legal redress.

Women who are victims of violence are often seen by police as over-reacting or as crazy. A witness who saw Teresa being terrorised by her husband on the day she was killed told the Coroner's Court:

> As we drove along the highway [having left the car park where they'd seen both Teresa and her husband in their respective

cars] we both agreed that we'd call the police at the next phone box. We had driven for some five to ten minutes when we saw a police car pulled over to the side of the road. We both got out of the car, and when I went over to the passenger side of the highway car, I said, "We have just been at the rest area, and I overheard a woman say that her husband had a rifle and was going to kill her". The driver then said, "did she seem a bit…" and he twirled his finger near his ear.

A discussion paper by the now-disbanded Police Complaints Authority dealing with the attitudes of the Victorian Police, though confined to victims of sexual violence, gives an insight into the attitude of police to female victims of crime generally. The paper comments that the attitudes of some members of the Victoria Police remain sexist, stereotyped and judgmental, and that these attitudes distress and alienate those female victims who come forward and discourage others from reporting crimes.[4]

Research undertaken in Victoria in the early 1980s, to compare the views of police with other professionals in relation to domestic violence, found that the police showed the least sympathy towards the victim, held the most stereotyped views of women and were more likely than the general public to harbour attitudes that supported and condoned domestic violence.[5]

Structured to discriminate

Internal police structures and culture work against women and children. In a recent report produced by the Victorian Federation of Community Legal Centres, police recruitment practice and the need for affirmative action for women in the police force are explored. The findings reveal that the Victorian police force unlawfully discriminates against women. This takes the form of:

> discrimination in recruitment and promotion along with sexual harassment and inequitable working conditions. Unlawful

discrimination in recruitment…ensures that those women who are successful in obtaining such employment remain only a small minority unable to challenge a status quo that largely excludes female experience and perspective. The marginal position of women in the police force is reinforced by discrimination in promotion which contributes to the small number of women in higher ranks of the force.[6]

The contradiction that exists between what police policy articulates and the service that women and children receive from the police can in part be seen as resulting from the hierarchical structure of the police force:

> The police force is a complex institution with many divisions staffed with officers with different responsibilities and levels of discretion. As a result of this there are many mediating forces between decisions at policy making levels and the implementation of the policies at street policing level…in practice it is often the rank and file officer who is the one to decide which policy applies to the reality she/he faces. In terms of everyday policing, it is the street level officer who is the major dynamic decision maker, making his or her decisions in the context of an elaborate hierarchy.[7]

Given this structural discrimination in the police force, and police role, ideology and culture, it comes as no surprise that the protection offered to women and children by the police is "conditional upon women meeting police notions of 'deservedness' and the circumstances of the attack meeting their definition of 'crime'. These notions are inevitably informed by misogyny, racism and classism and heterosexism of dominant social ideologies".[8]

While in recent years police policy has changed to a more pro-active stance (for example, the *Victoria Police Manual* 1.3.3, which directs police to arrest where sufficient evidence is available and to apply for an intervention order) police practice continues to lag dangerously behind policy. Instead of relying on the consistent application of police policy, women have to rely on the individual goodwill of attending officers.

This has serious consequences for women and children victims of male violence, potentially diluting the impact that any written law or stated police policy may have, by devolving power to street policing officers. In her study of male violence and the police Suzanne Hatty found that post-intervention interviews with officers "indicated several problematic behaviours and attitudes. These included non-enforcement of legislation and victim blaming".[9]

To understand how this occurs it is necessary to see that police culture distinguishes between supposed "real" police work — work which attracts both internal police reinforcement and public recognition — and supposed "non-police" work, such as administrative work at a desk or soft "social work" activities. This "non-police work" keeps police away from the "legitimate" police work of real crime fighting — where the police officer is depicted as "the crime fighting policeman — aggressive, suspicious and cynical, skilled in the use of weapons and the manipulation of physical means to maintain order".[10]

Police make a clear distinction between what they understand to be the public sphere where real crime occurs and where their intervention is unconditional, and the private sphere where intervention is conditional and based on their own ideas of what is acceptable behaviour.

In relation to the policing of male violence against women and children, police often see themselves in the role of mediator in family disputes. Suzanne Hatty found that:

> the majority of male police officers expressed disapproval regarding intervention in domestic violence. Despite the fact that domestic homicides form the largest category of homicides, the most common explanation offered by police for this negative response was that such intervention was not real police work, but was more probably the province of social workers.[11]

This is not a uniquely Australian experience; it has been substantiated through international research.[12]

A report in *Police Life*, the Victoria Police's glossy monthly, further highlights the distinction police seem to make between "real" police work and other work. Within the police force men are associated with the real crime fighting work, whereas women officers are largely confined to welfare, domestic and administrative roles. While women make up the majority of members within the Community Policing Squad (CPS) they are not represented, or poorly represented in what are considered "real" policing areas, such as the Criminal Investigation Branch (CIB), the Homicide Squad, the Special Operations Group and Search and Rescue.[13]

While the concentration of women in the CPS has drawn favourable responses from women, with Dr Rosemary Wearing finding that "women found the CPS to be more responsive to their needs",[14] it is a strong indictment of police attitudes and practice when real police work excludes domestic violence.

What the police can do

The police have as much power to act where there is domestic violence as they do when an assault occurs between two people who do not know each other.

Police have always had the power to enter private property, with force if necessary, to prevent a breach of the peace. This power comes from the Common Law which has been handed down by courts over time. If the police receive a phone call that there is violence or shouting then this is sufficient for them to form the "reasonable belief" that a breach of the peace is occurring or is about to occur. That phone call can be from the woman involved or a neighbour. Similarly, if police receive an anonymous phone call about "suspicious-looking" plants in a neighbour's backyard, this call is enough to justify obtaining a warrant to search the premises. Clearly, the police have — and exercise — the power to act on the basis of a phone call; nevertheless, they often say they don't have the power to act on a phone call about domestic violence.

The police are able to enter and remain on private premises with the "express or implied consent of an owner or occupier" whether or not another owner or occupier denies them entry.[15] This is a clear directive that the police are able to enter and stay on premises even if the man disagrees. The police have the power, under section 459A of the *Crimes Act 1958*, to search, enter and arrest without warrant if they have a reasonable belief that any of the following offences has occurred or is occurring: threat to kill, threat to inflict serious injury, causing serious injury, assault or threat to assault, or sexual assault. These offences describe the typical crime committed when there is violence against women and children in the home.

Under the *Crimes (Family Violence) Act 1987*, the police have the power to initiate an intervention order which directs a violent partner not to assault, harass or come near the woman and/or her children for up to a year. If there is a firearm involved, and police are satisfied that there are grounds for an intervention order, they have the power to enter homes and search for firearms without a warrant.[16]

In the past, Police Standing Orders directed police not to get involved in "domestic disputes". As a result of pressure from the public, women's refuges, Community Legal Centres and others, the *Police Manual* now clearly instructs them to "lay criminal charges even if the victim is reluctant". In addition, it states that police must take action and initiate intervention orders wherever the safety, welfare or property of a family member is endangered by another and the threat is ongoing. This may mean taking out an order without the agreement of the aggrieved family member. The manual also points out that restraining orders and intervention orders are not a substitute for the criminal law against assault.[17]

What are the police doing

The police would come in and ask what's wrong? The gun would be hidden. The kids would tell the police but my sister was too afraid to do anything. (Teresa's sister)

I called them, and they came almost an hour later. They took him into one room, and me into another. All they did was talk to us and try to calm him down. Then, they told me I could pack my things for five minutes, and took me and my three kids to the police station. We then went to the refuge. That was good, but they never charged him, and now we are pretty much homeless, and he is comfortable in our house. (Member of a domestic violence support group)

There is a large body of evidence to show that the police are not doing their job. Renata Alexander, a family law solicitor who has specialised in the area of domestic violence for a number of years, told a Victorian Committee Inquiry into Community Violence: "If police responded actively to calls for assistance in situations of domestic violence by laying criminal charges...some homicides may be prevented".[18] She said that police were unwilling to use their powers to investigate, often trivialised the violence and that they remained reluctant to intervene in domestic disputes, "misconceivedly viewing family violence as outside the sphere of criminal law and outside their area of intervention".[19]

A report by the Federation of Community Legal Centres revealed the failure of police in Victoria to attend and initiate action in reports of domestic violence: "...police still fail to attend. They fail to charge perpetrators even when police have been called to the premises on previous occasions. They fail to initiate intervention orders pursuant to the [*Crimes (Family Violence)*] Act. They fail to attend at the request of people who have obtained intervention orders, and even when they do attend, they fail to charge perpetrators who have breached the intervention orders".[20]

Community Legal Centres have subsequently reported that while police do attend numerous incidents of violence in the home, "there is little evidence that they consistently perform their duties as per the Force Circular Memo No. 91–5".[21]

Police inaction in cases of domestic violence is also documented in the report by Dr Rosemary Wearing, who analysed police statistics between 1987 and 1990. She found that in 72–5 per cent of cases where police claim there was violence used against a person, the members attending specified that no action was taken by them at the time. Where action was taken:

- arrests were made in six per cent of the cases (each year);
- warrants of arrest were issued in one per cent (1987–8) and 0.5 per cent (1989–90) of cases;
- summons to appear in court were issued in four per cent (1987–8) and 3.5 per cent (1989–90) of cases.[22]

Since November 1987, police in Victoria have been required to fill in a Family Incident Report Form (FIR) every time they attend a family violence call. The disbanded Victorian Law Reform Commission did a study of three thousand of these FIRs over the first four months of the new scheme.

> The FIR study showed that guns were present, threatened or used in 135 domestic incidents attended in the first four months and that in sixty-five per cent of cases, no prosecutorial steps were taken…the failure to prosecute or take steps, for example, to revoke a gun licence and seize the weapon, is cause for serious concern. In some of the cases where there were prosecutions, the prosecutions did not relate to the gun (e.g. in three cases where a gun had been threatened, the charge was drunkenness or breach of an intervention order)…other cases showed serious incompetence or neglect. Where one male perpetrator had a gun and a known history of violence, the constable concerned had decided that "the man would never use it".[23]

Research by Victoria Police found that police were:

> unaware or neglectful of their responsibilities and authorities in regard to firearms. Very few police made inquiries regarding the presence of firearms at "family incidents", the most frequent reason being "there was no need to ask". Yet this conclusion seemed to be based on observation such as "he seemed nice enough so we did not ask". The potential risk to both attending police and victims is clear and must be addressed.[24]

A NSW study into police attitudes was undertaken by researcher Suzanne Hatty. She conducted a number of interviews with police officers after they had attended domestic violence cases. One police officer described what happened when he attended a case of violence in the home:

> I spoke to the lady. She was very nervous, shaking and she explained it wasn't the first time her husband had abused her and physically hurt her...We were talking to her for about ten minutes before her husband came back in again and got a bit stroppy with the amount of time the police were taking talking to his wife. So we decided to leave, no questions asked.[25]

Another officer said that a woman rang him and reported that she had been grabbed by the throat and punched by her male partner, and that she did not want to live with him any more. She asked what advice he could give her. He told her about domestic violence orders and suggested that perhaps she should discuss it with her husband.[26]

When police attend a domestic violence call it is quite common for them to attempt mediation. They may advise the woman to leave with her children, effectively punishing her by making her homeless because of her partner's violence, rather than excluding the perpetrator from the home. Alternatively they may suggest she calls back if "something else happens".

They may take the man aside and tell him not to do it again, suggest he attend counselling or that they both attend marriage guidance. Sometimes they may advise the woman on intervention orders. Rarely do they lay charges and usually they leave soon after having arrived.

Furthermore, the police often refuse to assist women who are trying to separate from violent partners. The period immediately before and after separation is recognised as a particularly dangerous time,[27] and police assistance at this time is of vital importance in ensuring the safety of women and children.

Gatekeepers of the criminal justice system

Recent research has found that many women express strong dissatisfaction with the police response to male violence, a dissatisfaction very often based on their failure to arrest the violent male.[28]

The police have always had the power to act in situations of domestic violence. They have often excused their reluctance to do so on the grounds that they have a "discretion" not to charge and prosecute, despite the fact that police take an oath when they join the police force that they will enforce the law. Their tendency to exercise their discretion along the lines of their own prejudice has resulted in a whole class of people being excluded from the protection of the law: wives, de factos or girlfriends and daughters, or past wives, de factos or girlfriends.

This discretion, which translates as discrimination against women as a class, is compounded by prejudice against Aboriginal women, women from non-English-speaking backgrounds and working- and welfare-class women. With tragic consequences, police also discriminate against those women who most frequently call them for assistance about domestic violence. They are seen to be nuisances — out of control or weak.

The discretion police have in deciding whom to prosecute means that, effectively, they are gatekeepers of the legal system, diverting men who are violent from the criminal justice system.

Findings relating to the use of discretion among police officers has revealed that officers are unlikely to make an arrest when the offender has used violence against a female partner. A criminally violent man is arrested in only thirty-six per cent of cases in which women sustain physical injury. Injuries to the woman were found to be unrelated to the decision to arrest the male perpetrator. Police are more likely to arrest a man if he has sworn at them than if he has punched a woman.[29] In cases of violence between strangers, officers typically arrest the attacker regardless of the characteristics surrounding the crime.

Margaret's husband was taken away by the police on a number of occasions and locked up for being drunk. Despite his regular assaults on Margaret, he was charged with assault only once. It would appear that police see drunkenness as more serious than the violent assault of women.

Ann's experience is not uncommon. Her husband had talked about killing her on a number of occasions. Three months before he killed her, when Ann reported that he had broken down her door and bashed her, the police did not record the report. They did not charge him or inform her that she could do this, and they did not apply for an intervention order, or tell her about these or about restraining orders. Instead, they told her to call them if he did anything else. That "anything else" turned out to be killing her. If the police had acted when told of his violent behaviour and threats to kill, Ann might be alive now.

Anne knew her sister Teresa's life was in danger. She rang the police on the day her sister was murdered. She'd been ringing them for two weeks about her sister's safety. She gave them details of Teresa's car and Teresa's husband's car and told them he had a rifle. Anne pleaded with them to go on the road to protect her sister. They did not take any action before her sister's murder.

> I told them that he had a gun and was threatening to kill his family. I told them of the violence and the terror in the home, but they said they could do nothing unless Teresa made an official complaint or something happened.

> ...Why wasn't anything done when I reported it? They can't
> have followed her or she wouldn't be dead. I called them as
> soon as my sister hung up. They could have prevented it. If I'd
> rung up and said it was the PM there would have been a
> swamp of cars.

Not only do the police rarely lay charges against the perpetrators of criminal assault in the home, despite their
instructions to do so; they also rarely initiate intervention orders
on behalf of women who have been abused. Comments from
court registrars demonstrate this:

> A lot of police see the *Crimes (Family Violence) Act* and clerks
> as an easy way to clear troublesome people from the watch-
> house counter. It is classed too often as just a domestic, the
> easiest way out is to tell them to see the clerk of courts tomor-
> row or usually Monday morning.[30]

Effectively, violence against women is trivialised and men
who criminally assault their partners are not held accountable for
their behaviour.

Teresa's sister told us, "There was no intervention order.
This was despite the fact that the police had attended Teresa's
home on a number of occasions, in response to calls about his
violence. They knew he had a gun and that he had used it to
threaten Teresa".

In 1987, when the Victorian Government amended the
Crimes Act to include a provision for obtaining intervention
orders in the case of ongoing violence in the home, it was envis-
aged that the police would initiate the majority of orders so as
to relieve the victim of the psychological and financial pressure
of taking court action. This was made quite explicit at the time:
"[the] introduction of the new laws will provide police with the
powers that they need to prevent family violence and homicide".[31] However, one of the main problems with this legislation,
as with the powers police already possessed, is that it does nothing to tackle the continued reluctance of police to become

involved in "domestics".[32] Until now the police have initiated less than five per cent of these orders and are failing to arrest men for breaching them.[33]

When Chris called the police to report her husband's threats, she was advised to apply for an intervention order herself the next day, and in the meantime to stay overnight somewhere else. Her husband told her mother that "she was finished", but no action was taken by the police. When Vicki sought legal protection she was dismissed by the police: "It's just a piece of paper. If he wants to kill you he will".

Since the police rarely lay criminal charges or initiate intervention order applications, women are forced to pursue their own legal protection. This is a situation that other victims of violence rarely face. The legal system recognises that a crime against an individual is also a crime against society. For this reason the state has given the police, as its representatives, the responsibility and power to act where a crime is committed. This is also supposed to take away the fear, the risk of retribution and the burden of the legal prosecution from people who are already distressed by the crime committed against them.

When women and children are forced to initiate their own legal protection, the violence that they endure loses its status as a criminal offence. It is downgraded into the civil law area of family law, or into the quasi-criminal domain of restraining orders and intervention orders.

If the police had laid charges against Kay's husband for the abuse he inflicted on her and the threats he made to her and her children's lives, she would not have been forced to provide her own protection in the form of a restraining order. Police action would have moved the responsibility (and blame) for the legal action from the individual woman to the state. Instead, as Kay says, "I went to the police and sought advice about a restraining order against him, but I was too frightened to do anything about it for fear for my children's life". This fear is not unique. Many women live in constant fear, and endure continuing violence because the police do not lay charges against men who have criminally assaulted their partners.

When Vicki sought police assistance to go to her home to retrieve belongings, her sister Lorna told us, the police just advised her to "take a couple of mates".

One woman commented, "Is it any wonder I kept going back to him? With so little support and protection from the police, it is scary finishing that sort of relationship".[34]

Police make even less effort with women from non-English-speaking backgrounds. They often neglect to inquire if an interpreter is needed, and when they do seek to get an interpreter these attempts can be fraught with ignorance and prejudice, as in the case of a refuge worker who received a request from the police for an "Asian" interpreter. Police also make their own uninformed assessments about whether an interpreter is needed, based on whether they think they can understand the woman. They fail to consider that the woman may not understand them well enough.[35]

In these instances the woman from a non-English-speaking background is instantly disempowered, her situation is trivialised and the chances are that the outcome will be less than satisfactory from her point of view.

Why aren't they doing their job?

Police often explain their lack of action by claiming that they have no power to act if the violence has stopped by the time they arrive on the scene. This is in marked contrast to other types of crime, in which police investigation and arrest of suspects are seldom precluded by their failure to arrive in time to witness events. Other excuses are that too much paperwork is required for them to take action, that the victim doesn't want charges to be laid, that even if she does she'll change her mind in the morning and that it was only a quarrel which will blow over if left alone.

At a conference on domestic violence in 1982, an inspector of police stated that the police's main aim should be to prevent a tragedy, rather than to prosecute the offender after the damage is done.[36] This is a view rarely if ever expressed in relation to any other crime; further, it ignores the fact that by not prosecuting the offender the police are in fact giving him licence to further assault, and potentially to kill, women and children.

Police, like the wider community, appear to view domestic violence as less serious than other crimes and make a distinction between acts done in private and acts done in public. This results in a whole array of crimes against women going unacknowledged because most of these crimes occur in the privacy of the home. Violence in the home becomes a private family matter. An offender is not seen as a criminal or suspect but rather as someone who has "gone too far with the missus". Police have replied to criticism of their inaction by stating that "domestic violence is a complex problem which will not be solved by locking up every errant husband"[37] — despite the provisions of the Victorian *Crimes Act* and *Summary Offences Act* which prohibit physically violent behaviour regardless of the relationship between the victim and the assailant.

Many police make the judgement that "if it was really bad she would leave" and use this as an excuse for their inaction, ignoring the fact that as we have seen, there are many reasons why a woman is not able to leave a violent partner. Another evasive approach which effectively blames the woman for the violence is to write her off as crazy or hysterical — as did the police officers who made finger-twirling gestures when told by witnesses that Teresa had said her husband had a rifle and was going to kill her.

While police treat intervention as "the province of social workers",[38] in Victoria about forty per cent of the seventy homicides each year are domestic homicides.[39]

The consequences

I told my daughter to get help from the police or even a solicitor. Many times she told me that she would cope and be able to calm him down. She said she was too frightened to go to the police. (Teresa's father at the Coroner's Court)

The police had already visited Teresa's home on a number of occasions and taken no action against her husband who had been repeatedly violent towards her, including holding a gun at her head. It would appear that Teresa had no faith in the police and knew from experience that because they did nothing, calling them only made things worse.

Sue sought police assistance on three separate occasions but was told, "There is nothing we can do". On one occasion her husband attempted to strangle her. She scaled a large fence to get to the police, but they advised her not to bring assault charges in case of violent repercussions.

It has been found that:

> where the offender was female and information was available, in every case but one the homicide had been preceded by a history of battering towards the perpetrator, whilst in three quarters of the cases perpetrated by males the victim had previously been physically assaulted.[40]

It has also been found that in forty-eight per cent of spouse killings there has been at least one prior report to the police of violence.[41] This has been an opportunity for the police to intervene. Police failure to act according to their legal obligations leaves women and children in dangerous, sometimes lethal situations.

When they call the police, women want immediate protection from current and future violence. Police failure to attend when called and their failure, when they do attend, to use the criminal law, leaves women and their children vulnerable to further violence and death. On a broader level the message is given to the woman and the community that the violence is condoned and that the perpetrator will not be held accountable for his behaviour. The men have no reason to fear the state or the police when it is "only" their partners who are initiating action. They get the message that women have no support from the state or its agents in their claims.

Court registrars explain the consequences of police not taking action: "There was a woman who got an interim [intervention order] last year and she kept hassling the police who got sick of her — he killed her two weeks ago".[42] "We had one the other week where a lady with an intervention order was murdered. The police weren't acting on it as she'd made complaints on breaches."[43]

When a woman goes to the police and asks to lay charges, but they don't, what are her options? If women cannot rely on police protection in life-threatening situations some are forced to kill: either themselves, or in self-defence.[44]

Some don't call the police

There are women who are subject to violence in the home who will not call the police. For some this is because, on the basis of past experience or common knowledge, they doubt whether the police will do their job and provide them with adequate protection. In fact research into women's experience of the police found that those who had previously called them and had no action taken would not do so again.[45] Some women fear the repercussions if the police come and the offender is not charged: that they will be subject to further and perhaps exacerbated abuse from violent men who have received the message, implicit in police inaction, that it is all right to assault their partners and children.

Others have legitimate fears about what police intervention means for their communities. For instance, the high level of police violence and deaths in police custody experienced by Kooris makes it virtually impossible for Aboriginal women to seek the assistance of police. This creates a conflict for Aboriginal women who, on the one hand, are trying to stop violence against themselves, but who would not wish to be responsible for bringing further violence against their community by involving the police.

IN THE COURTS

Getting court orders

All the women and children in this book were subjected to abuse for many years before they were murdered. Most came into contact with the court system in the course of trying to stop the violence. Unfortunately women being abused face many obstacles in prosecuting the abuser or obtaining court orders that protect them and their children.

Magistrates' Courts are another first point of contact for many women seeking legal protection from violent partners. The attitudes court officials hold are similar to those held by police: court registrars, magistrates and judges often trivialise the violence, don't believe the woman, or attribute blame to her and excuse the behaviour of violent men. If the police have not taken action or have advised the woman to see the registrar, it is not unusual for the woman to be dissuaded from seeking legal protection by court staff.[46]

Vicki and her brother went to the court in an attempt to get a restraining order, having been told by the police that it was "just a piece of paper". The clerk of courts told her "There's nothing I can do". As a consequence Vicki did not pursue any further legal protection. Her sister told us that a day before Vicki was murdered, "I said to her 'Why don't you go to the police?' But she didn't know what to do, she had attempted to get a restraining order before".

Koori women and women from non-English-speaking backgrounds are further subjected to the racism of the legal system which actively prevents them from obtaining protection. For example, there is no automatic right to an interpreter for women whose first language is not English.[47] Koori women are faced with the whole history of discrimination by the dominant legal system towards Aboriginal people in this country.

Women being abused are often put in further danger by inadequate enforcement of restraining and intervention orders. Many families and friends we spoke to believe that court orders which were inadequately enforced gave the offender a licence to further abuse, and that adequate enforcement early in the piece might have prevented the violence from escalating. Many women have so little faith in the legal system that they do not pursue their rights. Jill didn't try to get an intervention order because Keith's abuse consisted mostly of emotional abuse and threats, and she doubted whether the police or the courts would take notice of that.

A complicating factor for women in getting protective orders is the need to deal with their husbands and partners in relation to family law matters such as access, custody and property. Although Gene successfully obtained an intervention order against her husband, after it expired she was afraid to renew it for fear he would deny her access to her daughter. Women are often fearful of retribution from their violent partners if they try to use the legal system to get protection. This is a realistic assessment for a woman to make, since the legal system obviously cannot hope to prevent all violence; but it is also a reflection of the history of inadequate responses from police, lawyers and courts. Women who are being abused cannot afford the risk of legal action if the response of the police and courts is uncertain. This creates a climate in which abused women often do not report the violence or seek protection.

Access and custody

Especially in custody children are treated as commodities. (CHRIS)

Another reason for having contact with the court system occurs after separation when Family Court proceedings for custody and access begin. Many of the women whose stories appear in this book found that the Family Court actively reinforced attitudes that trivialised the violence they had endured and shifted the responsibility away from the offender.

Access proved to be fatal for several of the women and children in this book. Paul and Lisa were killed by their father while on an access visit, Gene was killed by her ex-husband when she went to collect her daughter for access, Christine was killed when her husband was at her house for an access visit to the children. Her sister Carmel says:

> My sister's murder was committed at an access visit ordered by the Family Court. She had applied for an urgent hearing and had moved five times with him pursuing her with a gun. The court ordered that she get a "normal" home for her children and that she give him access. The last time I spoke to her she told me what she had arranged. I remember getting panicky and telling her not to do it. She could not break the court order if she wanted to protect her children and have custody of them in the long term. Despite her better judgement she complied with the order. It cost her her life.

Despite Ann giving evidence in court that her husband had repeatedly assaulted her in front of her children, her ex-husband was granted weekly overnight access. This placed Ann in constant fear as he picked up and dropped off the children from her place. And these are by no means isolated cases.

The Family Court must take seriously pleas for protection where women are declaring their fear for their children and themselves because of the violence and threats they have experienced. There is a strong case for access to be denied to men who are violent towards either their partner or children.

Some of the women referred to in this book did not go through Family Court proceedings for custody or access because they were afraid of the consequences for themselves and their children. Some women left their children with their ex-partners because of his threats to harm the children or his claims that he could completely deny her contact. On separation Gene was forced to leave her 21-month-old daughter with her husband. She didn't contest custody because her husband threatened to kill both her and her daughter if she attempted to take her away from him. Gene was extremely upset about leaving her daughter but she was in such fear that she agreed. Kay did not seek a custody order in court to formalise custody of Laurell and Michael because her husband told her that if she went to the police or tried to stop him seeing the kids he would kill both children. He eventually murdered Laurell during a dispute with Kay over custody.

Many men intimidate their partners with spurious legal claims such as "the courts will never give you custody or access because you are a bad mother". We were told by a family member that when Kay indicated she was leaving, her ex-husband threatened that she would "never get the children". She left the children with him for nine months because of this threat.

Many supposed agreements on access, custody and property come about through coercion of the woman because of her fear and experiences of violence. When decisions are made about access the safety of women and children is not given sufficient consideration. Rather, the father's rights are given priority. The court can, however, order supervised access or supervised "hand-overs": access or hand-over arranged to take place in the presence of a third party. The grounds for supervised access are supposed to be either danger to the child, or danger and threats of abduction — that the child won't be returned after access. The types of danger the court would consider include violent behaviour, either inflicted on the child or in the presence of the child;

threats to harm the child; or alcohol or drug-addicted behaviour considered to be dangerous to the child. The court is supposed to look after the best interests of the child in making this decision. Anecdotal evidence indicates that supervised access and supervised hand-overs are rarely stipulated by the court.

The pressure on women not to contest custody and access is often subtle, and is enforced by attitudes in the community that are upheld by the courts. Many women, for example, believe that it is important that children maintain contact with their father even when this places them in a dangerous situation. Chris told us, "I'd read about cases like this and thought poor man, not allowed to see his kids. I wanted to do the right thing". Even for those who have experienced the danger and threats, it is hard to believe that the children could be killed by their father. Many other family members spoke of this view that it was the "right thing to do".

Chris was advised by the Family Court counsellors to allow her ex-husband access to their children despite his violence towards her and the children. The court ordered that she provide access. As she says, "I never felt that there was any danger to the children. You just don't expect it".

Access to abuse

Workers at the Victorian Domestic Violence and Incest Resource Centre and the Victorian Refuge Program report that exposure of children to all kinds of violence — sexual, physical and emotional — is prevalent on access visits, as are threats, harassment and assaults against their mothers. Little research has been done into how widespread the incidence of "access abuse" is; however, there is enough anecdotal evidence from family lawyers, refuge and other domestic violence and sexual assault workers to be of grave concern.

The Family Court needs to take into consideration the safety and well-being of children in the making of access and custody orders. While the Family Court purports — and is in fact required — to uphold the best interests of the child in custody and access disputes, doubt has been cast on whether this is really the case, where children have been exposed to continued violence on access visits.

In its submission to the 1991 inquiry into the operation of the *Family Law Act*, the National Committee on Violence against Women made the following points: "It is not and can never be in the best interests of a child to be exposed to violence";[48] and, "The father who abuses, beats, denigrates, rapes, assaults and is generally violent towards the mother of his children does not promote the welfare of his children and his behaviour cannot ever be in the best interests of a child'.[49] In the national research conducted by Elliott and Shanahan in 1988 interviewees were concerned that "the Family Court is reluctant to deny access to a violent or sexually abusive father",[50] and a family law solicitor told the researchers that "the Family Court does not take into account the damage caused to children when determining custody and access rights of fathers. Children are often justifiably frightened of their fathers".[51]

The Family Court is not supposed to take a punitive approach to settling cases or to apportion fault or blame. However, the National Committee on Violence against Women has noted the Family Court's tendency, in its endeavour to remove guilt, innocence or fault from custody, guardianship and access disputes, to avoid taking a firm stance to "positively prohibit and denounce violence as contrary to the best interests of the child".[52] It is important that considerations of the best interests of children should not be perceived as a reintroduction of fault.

Property and maintenance

In 1986, the Institute of Family Studies published a study into the relative outcomes of property settlements for men and women. The study found that the standard of living for non-custodial parents, mostly men, had increased markedly, while that of the mothers and children had decreased compared to the pre-divorce situation.[53] The introduction of the Child Support Scheme has altered this situation to some extent, in that it is now easier to collect maintenance; however women and children who exist on the Sole Parent's Pension or inadequate maintenance continue to live in poverty.

Women often forego what they are legally entitled to because of the abuse by their partners. Ann considered applying to the court for more maintenance, but her husband told her sister, "If she goes for more maintenance I'll take those kids, right, and I'll fix her. I won't bring the kids back when I have them of a weekend".

Property and maintenance proceedings can be a particularly dangerous time for women. A family member said, "There were two main factors involved in Mick killing Ann. He had lost control of her. Secondly, she was going to court for her fair share of marital property and for a more reasonable amount of maintenance".

Some women decide to settle as quickly as possible even if it means settling for less because of the urgent need for funds to re-establish themselves. Many settle for much less property than they are entitled to, hoping that it will prevent further violence or dissuade their violent partner from seeking custody.

A family member told us that despite the fact that Ann was entitled to more for herself and the children, she agreed to a fifty-fifty property settlement "to keep the peace". Ann's husband killed her three days before the Family Court hearing which was to settle their property. She questions why he never bothered to prepare for that hearing.

Two of the offenders in this book ensured that the property would be destroyed. Chris's husband burnt down their house after killing the children; and Sue's husband smashed up the house to the point of demolition before killing her, in case she survived.

CHAPTER FIVE

After the killing — the legal system

✳

BEFORE THE TRIAL

She wasn't portrayed as a person who had rights or feelings — she was just dead. It was almost as if she didn't matter... The only conclusion you can reach is that women's lives aren't worth very much. (JUDY)

Men look around and say to themselves, that's okay, I'll do it too, nothing will happen to me. Everyone else gets off — I will too. This allows and encourages men to keep being violent. (MARY)

The legal system prides itself on being fair and just, but it must be remembered that it is largely premised on values which protect and serve the interests of white, male, middle-class culture. The experiences of the criminal justice system and opinions of the family members and friends in this book raise questions about whether justice is being done for women and children.

Following the killings of these women and children the legal system responded with investigation, the laying of charges and the trial of the offender. This brought surviving family members and friends into contact with the Coroner's Court, the Magistrates' Court and the Supreme Court. A number of the surviving families also had to deal with the offender's application for custody of the children through the Family Court, and surviving mothers had to face the offender again during property settlement proceedings.

To find out how the legal system dealt with the killings we looked at the homicide squad summaries and the coronial, committal and Supreme Court transcripts, where available, as well as interviewing families and friends. The theme already established throughout this book — of the underlying belief systems and attitudes which inform the practice of the various players in the legal system, to the detriment of the victims and survivors of male violence in the home — is echoed in this chapter. The violence has been trivialised and privatised not only when women have sought protection for themselves and their children, but also after the murder. Rarely is the offender held responsible for his actions.

After the killing, the first contact with the law comes when police interview witnesses and the suspect. During this phase the police are gathering information and evidence to determine whether they will lay charges. The Magistrates' Court then holds a committal hearing, to determine whether there is a case to be heard for either murder or manslaughter (depending on the initial charge) based on the evidence put forward by the Director of Public Prosecutions (DPP) and the police. The initial charge can be altered either before or during the committal hearing.

When someone has died other than from natural causes or where there is doubt as to the cause of death, the Coroner holds an inquiry to determine the cause of death, not to decide on criminal liability. The Coroner's inquiry usually happens after the committal hearing. The trial occurs after both sides have prepared their cases and the matter has been timetabled to be heard in the Supreme Court.

In this chapter we detail these processes further in the light of the experiences of the families and friends of the women and children who were killed.

Initial police investigations

Family members and friends described varying experiences with the homicide squad. Some families found them, as Judy did, "very supportive and sympathetic, particularly with my parents". Others were not happy for a number of reasons and felt that the police had not always done their job properly during their investigations. Often the family had not been given adequate information. Some family members and friends were fearful of the defendant and yet police did not notify them when he was released on bail. They spoke of being "the last to know" and said that the homicide squad told them little.

They also felt that the police did not gather enough evidence, particularly about the prior violence by the accused towards the victim. Of those we interviewed, many were critical that there was little questioning of witnesses about prior domestic violence.[1] In some of the cases where family and friends were not questioned about the circumstances of the woman's death, they believe that their evidence would have revealed how premeditated the killing was. A member of Ann's family recalled a number of such actions and statements by Ann's ex-husband — for example, he often told family members, "If I can't have her nobody else will" — and she believes that other circumstantial evidence was not investigated fully. "No fingerprints or scrapings under fingernails were taken which may have shed light or shed doubt on his claim that he acted in self-defence."

Nona, a friend of Gene's, similarly believes that in Gene's case many relevant facts were omitted from the initial investigation which would have shown that the killing was premeditated. For example, Schembri had arranged for the child not to be present despite having told Gene she would be given access, and he had made no preparations for the property settlement hearing which was to take place the week after he killed her. Another friend, Nona, took the initiative to inform the DPP of other information the police had not investigated but found that the DPP wasn't interested. Nona said, "There were circumstances

Banner made for the 1989 Domestic Murders Commemoration

Laurell

Lisa

Paul

Card from Paul and Lisa to Chris

Drawing by Christine Boyce

that clearly indicated his pre-planning that never came up in court". The police investigation into Gene's death did not reveal the prior violence and threats to kill her. Rosa, who had lived with Gene and had witnessed Gene's husband's violence towards her, was not interviewed by police. Rosa told the media about this history. One journalist concluded that "The police investigation did not include any details of the troubled Schembri marriage. Homicide detectives and the Director of Public Prosecutions decided that there was no premeditation involved".[2]

Carmel said:

> My sister was murdered at the same time as the Walsh Street police shootings. The homicide squad were busy investigating this and delegated the investigation of my sister's murder to a junior CIB detective on his first homicide case. The police officer did what he could, but before the committal and before the case I tried to get access to the prosecutor to talk about the case, what they were arguing, what evidence was required etc. I was sure they were not properly prepared. I believe that the resources allocated at the time reflected the seriousness with which the police saw her murder.

Chris made a statement to the police soon after her children had been killed. After the initial shock, and having given her first statement to the police, she wanted to give further information. The police refused to take further statements. She was told that they had enough evidence. She wanted to tell them about his previous violence. She says that when she gave her first statement it was only hours after being told that her children had been stabbed and had their skulls smashed and that her first reaction to the brutality of the murders was that he was just crazy. Later she had time to reflect on his previous violence to her and her children. She told us, "I was dazed thinking he must have been crazy. I don't think he was crazy. Later things came together when I thought about my married life".

The homicide file notes, which are a summary of the initial police investigation, rarely indicate the existence of charges, intervention or restraining orders or any previous domestic violence history. It has been argued that the reason past domestic violence history is not documented in initial police investigations is that it is presumed that it will not be allowed in court. However, the police approach is inconsistent — some police don't investigate this history while others do; and it appears routine to gather information about the victims' prior behaviour, which would contradict such reasoning. In our opinion, it is police attitudes that determine whether such enquiries are made.

The police interview with the accused, made soon after the killing, is regarded in law as providing the most truthful and accurate account of what happened. However it is apparent from our interviews with family members that the type of questions asked has a bearing on the answers given.[3] In one case, where the accused was asked by the police, "Did you argue very often?" a direct question about past violence might have prompted different answers.

In Gene's case, her husband alleged that she slapped his face and yelled at him and that this explained why he strangled her to death. The DPP appeared to accept this explanation. Gene's friends believe that the interviewing police officer reinforced his own belief that her husband had lost control. The police didn't ask him whether he had previously threatened and assaulted her, and in the Supreme Court Gene's husband denied that he had ever been violent toward her. The prosecution did not challenge his denial. It seems that investigating police may not inquire about previous domestic violence because they have already made their own judgement as to the circumstances and motive.

Although there is rarely an attempt to make connections between past violence inflicted on a woman and her killing, there is often a search to find excuses for a man's violence. Motives such as jealousy, arguments, separation or finances are suggested. There is a disproportionate focus by police on the woman's behaviour or on other events, rather than the offender's past behaviour.

Deciding on the charge

The accused in most homicides are initially charged with murder, but few trials result in a murder conviction. The Law Reform Commission's study of Victorian homicides found that out of 243 cases committed to trial for murder, only fifty-seven (23.5 per cent) resulted in a murder conviction. Forty-five per cent of those charged with murder were convicted of manslaughter.[4]

The police initially decide the charge, usually in consultation with the Director of Public Prosecutions. The magistrate at the committal hearing decides if there is enough evidence for the case to go to trial and on what charge. The DPP is not bound by the decision of the committal magistrate and may change the charge, for example, if they consider that there is little chance of a conviction being secured for the initial charges. At this stage it is common for the accused to offer, or be offered, the lesser charge of manslaughter in return for pleading guilty. Alternatively, the jury has the power to convict the killer of manslaughter even though the charge was murder.

In the homicides of Gene, Vicki, Margaret, Mirela and Christine, either the accused was offered a manslaughter charge or the jury convicted him of manslaughter on an original charge of murder; Sue's and Teresa's killers suicided and so no charges were laid; in the cases of Jill, Laurell and Paul and Lisa the charge and the conviction were murder.

The families we interviewed were not happy with the decisions about the charges. They believe that the DPP, in particular, has little accountability to the public in their decision to charge an accused with manslaughter rather than murder. It was the view of many family members that the DPP is much too readily inclined to charge an accused with manslaughter in a domestic killing as compared with other homicide cases, and that the decision to charge with manslaughter is either a readiness to accept that women provoke domestic killings, or simple expediency.

After Gene was killed a public demonstration was organised to express outrage at the decision to reduce the charge against her ex-husband from murder to manslaughter. Spokeswoman Melba Marginson said, "We are not happy over the acceptance of the crown of the plea for manslaughter because we believe it was really murder…We are deeply saddened by the fact that this has happened. How many years is a life worth?"[5]

Many people felt that the police and the DPP assumed that because Gene allegedly slapped her ex-husband, this justified reducing the charge from murder to manslaughter. They believed that the police decided this action amounted to a legal defence of provocation and consequently didn't investigate the case properly. Barrister Jocelynne Scutt, invited by the Victorian Filipino community to speak about Gene's case at a forum in 1990, expressed the view that there should be a law requiring any reduction in charge instigated by the DPP to be explained by way of statement to the court at trial. This would then be on public record, ensuring that it could be challenged.

Some families and friends were not satisfied with the decisions of committal magistrates to reduce the charges, particularly where the issue of self-defence was raised to justify the killing. The legal definition of self-defence is that a person who is unlawfully assaulted is justified in causing death to their assailant if they believed on reasonable grounds that it was necessary to act as they did in order to defend themselves.[6] They need not have believed that they would be killed.

Ann's ex-husband strangled her in what he claimed was self-defence, alleging that Ann had attacked him with a knife to the shoulder. This defence was accepted. Her sister Mary told us, "At the committal hearing the prosecutor wanted to make the charge murder but the magistrate said that it should be manslaughter".

In Mirela's case, the police sought psychiatric evidence but still charged her husband with murder. They opposed the option of committal to a psychiatric institution instead of jail, indicating that they held him responsible for his own actions. However at the hearing his defence lawyer argued that his actions were due to insanity and the magistrate reduced the charge to manslaughter.

Vicki's ex-de facto was initially charged with murder but at his committal he attempted to have the charge reduced to manslaughter because of his "heavy drinking and her provocation" (that she swore at him and had left him). The magistrate ordered that he be tried for murder because of evidence from three different sources alleging that he had had a prior intention to kill her. He *was* tried for murder, but the jury accepted that there had been legal provocation and convicted him of manslaughter. "It was the verdict rather than the sentence we are angry about", said Vicki's brother. "...of course four years [the actual duration of incarceration] seemed a paltry sentence; however the verdict of manslaughter was the fundamental problem. Here the rights of women and the responsibilities of men were defined in such a way as to leave us with a great deal to worry about."

Bail

The granting of bail is an important issue for the families and friends of murdered women and children. Many of the people we talked to were extremely fearful of the accused because he saw them as taking "her side" and providing police with information after the killing. They believed he was capable of inflicting further violence — in some cases immediate family and friends had already been threatened or abused by the accused, giving further foundation to their fears. The fact that he knew them well made them feel especially vulnerable to harassment, but this was rarely even considered when bail conditions were being set.

In Gene's case, for example, the granting of bail made witnesses scared to come forward. In Jill's case, her ex-husband was on bail for two years. Her sister said, "I lived in terrible fear that he would kill me, as he knew that I had encouraged Jill to leave him for years". According to her sister Mary, Ann's family felt threatened by Ann's killer to the extent that they sought an intervention order.

Factors taken into account by a magistrate or judge in deciding whether a person gets bail are:
- the nature and seriousness of the offence
- the risk to witnesses and members of the public
- the likelihood of reoffending
- the criminal record of the accused
- protection of the accused
- the likelihood of the accused absconding[7]

"Good character" is also taken into account in bail applications. Jill's ex-husband was granted bail on the basis of a character reference from a mayor. His character was so untarnished by the murder that his mates held a chook raffle at the pub to raise money for bail.

THE TRIAL

Obviously when you're dead you can't speak out, and the legal system doesn't provide you with a voice. (HELEN)

The court system does not allow for the jury to recognise that the murdered woman had a life that was unjustly taken from her. She hardly even gets a mention. (JUDY)

We felt let down by the legal system. (DONNA and LORNA)

The court system raised some of the strongest and most irate comments from the families and friends we interviewed. The main criticisms primarily concerned the lack of justice for those who were killed, the lack of opportunity for the families to respond to the character assassinations and lies they had to listen to as part of the defence case, and the conspiracy of silence surrounding the prior violence the women and children who were killed had experienced at the hands of the defendant. They were also distressed where convictions were made on reduced charges, and by the level of sentences handed down.

Chris said, "the legal system in this country has decreased the value of life…He used to scoff at it and comment on how easy it was to kill someone and get away with it. Judges, too, seem too quick to want to give criminals a second chance, yet those same murderers do not do the same for their victims…The whole legal system needs to be overhauled to allow the real truth to be known".

In the court foyer after the verdict in the trial of Peter Keogh was handed down, Lorna Cleary cried out "Do you know what you've done?" Later she put it this way:

> It was as if my daughter had done something wrong. This man who cried when giving unsworn evidence had harassed Vicki before and after she left him. She did nothing to him. She just wanted to get on with her life. He refused to let her do that, yet when it came to making a decision the jury accepted the defence of provocation. It was so wrong.

For most families the experience of being in court was one they will never forget. It was not the macabre detail of the death or the clinical examination of the events that shocked them, but the sheer injustice and total inadequacy of the legal system's response to the death of these women and children.

How the story gets told — police as witnesses

At the trial, what occurred is conveyed secondhand by whatever witnesses the prosecution decides to call. It seemed from the transcripts we examined that witnesses were rarely called. Instead, police officers told the court about their observations and findings based on their assessment of what people told them in interviews. The story of the woman who has been murdered is told largely by the police, who act as witnesses, and by the accused. This inevitably means that her experience is portrayed in a selective and often biased manner. In court the opinions offered by police are often highly influential and are given considerable weight. In some of the cases police were asked questions that gave professional credibility to what could really only have been superficial, subjective and, frequently, biased opinions. In Gene's case, a police officer was asked these questions:

- Was it clear to you that he was very much devoted to his daughter?
- Was she the love of his life?
- Was the accused concerned with his daughter's exposure to the personal lifestyle of the deceased?

Apart from the fact that police officers are unlikely to have known either the victim or the accused, such questioning is not based on any expertise that the police have on love and devotion. Such areas of questioning are irrelevant, and too-readily invite their own prejudices about the roles of men and women, and attitudes to domestic violence. In domestic murder cases it is particularly damaging because the defence is usually keen to develop a stereotype to explain the accused's behaviour — for example, that he was a devoted father who killed for love.

Killers not to blame

The family members and friends also spoke of what they believed was an exaggerated sympathy and bias shown by the barristers, the judge and the jury in favour of the accused, shifting the responsibility away from him to women, other people or circumstances.

Jill's sister Judy told us, "The court case lasted two and a half weeks and during this time the counsel for the defence built up a tremendous amount of sympathy for this poor man who just couldn't cope with the emotional trauma of separation from his wife".

In court, Gene's ex-husband obtained sympathy because, in the words of a defence barrister, "He was so naive he watched a TV program about happiness and wonderful marriages and not only believed it, but acted on it". Ann's sister Mary told us, "Much of the defence strategy was on suggesting to all witnesses that Mick was a placid and non-violent man". Judy spoke of:

> the sympathy that society gives to men who kill their part-
> ners. This was evident during Keith's trial. The jury came back
> and asked the judge if they could find him guilty of
> manslaughter instead of murder. Luckily they couldn't. They
> looked at photos of her dead body and yet felt sympathy for
> her killer.

Another strategy used by defence lawyers was blaming other people for the murder — people who weren't even there. In Vicki's case part of the defence strategy was to blame the accused's "possessive" mother for his actions when, as Donna and Lorna said, "the poor woman wasn't even there to defend her-self". In contrast, Chris's ex-husband blamed Chris's mother for not being "family enough" to him. Kay remarked that "the defence were very confused. Everyone else got blamed but Den-nis…The defence lawyer tried to say Laurell wasn't a nice little girl — as if that mattered — and it wasn't true anyway".

Some women are seen as deserving the violence, and once again the blame is shifted away from the killer. In two of the cases we looked at, the court focused on the woman's work in the sex industry as if it in some way explained her murder, despite the fact that both the men who killed these women knew about their work and benefited from it. "The defence painted her as a terribly wicked woman", said one family member, "but he knew her profession before he married her".

The absent witnesses — women and children

Many families and friends were distressed that the deceased women's stories were not told, and that therefore much of what the accused said wasn't challenged. As Mary said, "During the trial there was not much said about Ann". "The prosecution put you on the stand", said Kay, "and then they tear you to shreds. It's all question and answer — so you don't get to tell how it is". Vicki's mother said,

> What I can't understand is that his friends were asked their opinion of the relationship yet we weren't allowed to get up and say anything. There was no-one there to give Vic a character reference, no-one to get up and say, look despite what you've heard just let us tell you a little bit about her, so you understand what sort of a person she was.

The absent history — previous violence ignored

Many of those we interviewed felt that the prosecutor could have been more active in refuting character assassinations of the dead women and children, and more active in raising relevant issues. Chris told us, "I wrote notes to the clerk and the prosecutor when lies came up. It is so hard to sit there and listen to all the lies. It was particularly hard on my mother because she was blamed". She added, "The prosecutor said very little during court. He said appropriate things at times but could have said a lot more".

In Gene's case the assertion by the defence that there was no previous physical violence was not challenged by the prosecutor even though there was evidence available. Her ex-husband's previous violence towards her was not raised by the prosecutor, except for one witness's evidence that he had sent her a newspaper clipping about the domestic murder of a Filipina and expressed sympathy for the killer. The judge did indicate that he viewed this as a previous threat and questioned the defence about it on a number of occasions; however it was not pursued by the prosecutor, nor ultimately by the judge.

Ann's sister said, "I didn't think the prosecutor was supportive or interested in what I had to say. He suggested that 'lay people do not understand the court procedure' when I was upset that I didn't get to tell her story". As a result, "many important issues were not raised in the trial".

Families were extremely angry that an accused would claim his actions were entirely unpremeditated when clearly there had been a long history of violence. This is the case in most domestic murders, and yet rarely is a prior history of violence mentioned in court.

Some lawyers argue that past history of domestic violence should not be mentioned in court because it prejudices the chances of the accused who is, after all, being tried for the murder and not for his past behaviour. Others suggest that such evidence can be introduced, particularly to challenge a defence of provocation: that the previous domestic history is relevant where the accused relies so heavily on portraying his actions as spontaneous, atypical and provoked. In the absence of information in court about prior domestic violence, the focus is on the woman's behaviour and on finding justifications for the murder. This approach fails to recognise the continuum of violence, in which murder is simply the end point.

But whether past domestic violence can be introduced as evidence in court is not just a matter of legal uncertainty. It seems to family and friends, and to the Women's Coalition Against Family Violence, that the reasons it is not mentioned are to do with lawyers' and judges' attitudes towards domestic violence. Vicki's brother was told by the prosecution that "evidence about past violence has to be of like kind and that the act of taking a knife and killing her was of considerable difference to belting her occasionally".[8]

Ann's family believe that Ann's alleged attack on her ex-husband would not have been as readily accepted by the jury if they had been aware of his past history of violence against her.

(They also noted that while the court ignored the past history of violence, it was willing to speculate about her behaviour by asking her daughter whether Ann "saw any men" while her parents were married.)

In the rare instances in which past violence is introduced as evidence, the physical abuse will often be trivialised and the psychological, emotional or sexual abuse accompanying it, including death threats, will be ignored.

Some families and friends spoke of how the defence barrister focused on justifications for the murder and said that there was little challenge to this by the prosecutor or the judge. Chris was available to give evidence about her ex-husband's prior violence and yet it was not raised. "I felt that his prior history of violence should have been raised in court. Instead the defence claimed that it was the separation that caused the distress and led to the murders."

In Gene's case, the failure to mention any past violence meant that her action in leaving her child with him (out of fear) could not be explained. Her friend Nona said, "She was wrongly painted as a flirt who walked out on him and left him literally holding the baby. The defence emphasised the fact that he had custody of such a young child. It is the view of her friends that this helped him get a light sentence".

In Vicki's case, as in many others, the court heard that the killer had no intention of killing her because he loved her. The fact that Peter Keogh had made what Vicki described as threatening phone calls to her at work was never mentioned. Lorna Cleary said that had she "been able to tell the court what my daughter told me, Keogh's claim that he loved her would have looked very sick. I just wished I could tell the jury what I knew".

The fact that the past violence of the killer towards his partner is not raised enables the defence to claim not only that love was present in the relationship, but furthermore, in the ultimate twist, that it was responsible for the murder. In Christine's case, her sister said, "No domestic violence was introduced, nor was the history of their relationship. The defence claimed that 'love had pulled the trigger'". In the absence of past domestic violence history, most cases focus attention on what happened just before the killing. The context is lost, the blame is shifted, and the circumstances of the murder distorted.

In Vicki's case, the court focused on her allegedly swearing at Keogh immediately prior to the murder. In Christine's case, an argument over the children was said to have provoked her ex-husband to shoot her three times in the neck and chest, in their presence. For Jill, the focus of the evidence was Keith's distress at their separation and his explanation that if he couldn't have her, then no-one else could. For Mirela, in the absence of evidence about his years of abuse, the court focused on her agreeing to her husband being released from psychiatric care, and on whether he was mad. Ironically, a psychiatrist told the court: "I was highly surprised the crime happened. I felt the wife was in control at home".

For many of the women, this invisible previous history included death threats. Chris told us, "The court found that there had been little premeditation on his part but it was from the very first day of our separation that he would say over the phone that he knew what the end would be, that I did not know what sort of person he was. The way he would say those things would send a chill down my spine". Vicki's brother said, "The jury was confronted with a prior threat of murder, but he was still found guilty of manslaughter".

In many cases previous violence was not allowed to be mentioned because of the "hearsay" rule. This is a rule of evidence that says witnesses can only give evidence about things they have seen or heard personally and not what they have been told about by other people. It is considered difficult to test the truth of the evidence by cross-examination if the witness hasn't actually seen what happened. Unfortunately, the nature of domestic violence is such that there are rarely witnesses to it — the victim may tell other people of the violence, but they are unlikely actually to be there at the time. Christine's ex-husband,

111

for example, broke her nose and jaw and threatened to kill her, but that information was inadmissible because no-one saw it happen. This lack of witnesses is common enough, but it is compounded by official inaction in response to incidents of domestic violence. There is often little evidence about previous violence because it is not documented by police, hospital workers and other professionals. The fact that the deceased was the only witness to the abuse makes it difficult in some cases for this history to come out.

Christine's sister Carmel and her friend conclude, "Justice is not served when the prosecution cannot mention previous violence of the accused toward the victim or give a context to the so-called 'provocative' acts".

The use of race and culture as a defence.

It was evident from our interviews, and particularly from the media reports we analysed, that racial stereotyping is often used in domestic murder cases to defend the actions of the accused. In one of the cases we looked at the media described the killer as an "old-fashioned Italian". The family's view, as expressed by Anne, was: "He could do whatever he wanted to do. Where does that fit with tradition?"

In the trial of Gene's ex-husband many of her friends were appalled by what they regarded as an uncritical acceptance by the court of a combined racist and sexist justification for his killing. His assertion that he had been exploited gained hold in the court and the media because of sexist and racist assumptions of what a Filipina woman should be. In court, the defence introduced a sociological study to assert that Gene's ex-husband expected his wife to be, amongst other things, "beautiful, modest, timid and devoted to family and domestic life". The contrast between this stereotype and Gene's real personality was used to support his assertion that she had used him to gain a passport.

Similarly, Chris believes her husband's racial background (he is Kenyan) was used unfairly to justify his violence. She prepared information for the prosecutor on Kenyan culture after hearing that the defence would be using cultural expectations as an excuse during a plea for leniency. She believes that in the defence case cultural factors were distorted and that culture should not be used as an excuse. She commented that he wasn't very traditional, yet in court his traditional values were strongly asserted.

The court also heard evidence from a Nigerian "expert" on mothers-in-law as part of Simon's defence. Chris told us that Kenyan customs are different from Nigerian, and although this difference was brought out in court, she believes that the evidence about Nigerian culture was still taken into account and accepted — as though he was Nigerian, and as though this was an adequate account of his actions.

LEGAL DEFENCES

> Laws relating to self-defence or provocation in cases of domestic killing may be "neutral", or apparently so. It is when they are analysed, or interpreted by courts to the disadvantage of women that neutrality is seen to be lacking.[9]

In a murder case the accused, if not pleading guilty, can use two types of defence:
- a full defence such as self-defence or insanity. If a full defence is successful the accused is found not guilty. A successful insanity defence puts the offender in a psychiatric institution;
  or
- a partial defence such as provocation. A successful partial defence reduces the conviction from murder to manslaughter.

Most domestic murder cases result in a conviction of manslaughter. This is either because the legal defence of provocation is successfully raised in court or because the police and the DPP think that a plea of provocation would probably be successful, so they offer the accused the opportunity to plead guilty to manslaughter. Self-defence and insanity defences are also used but are not as commonly argued as provocation.

A legal defence of provocation was raised in a number of the cases we looked at. Even where it wasn't used as a legal defence, the notion of the woman supposedly provoking her own killing came up.

In Mirela's and Ann's cases, although insanity and self-defence were the defences raised they were argued similarly to the cases where provocation was argued. Witnesses were questioned about the character of the dead woman, quite clearly to establish that she had in some way contributed to her own death. In the cases concerning the killings of Laurell and Jill, while provocation was not formally raised there was a heavy emphasis, particularly in sentencing, on these murders being "crimes of passion" and being provoked by circumstances beyond the offenders' control.

Provocation

Provocation [the legal defence] refers to sudden loss of self-control by reason of provocative behaviour and actions which might have been perpetrated by an ordinary person in the position of the accused. (Justice Vincent, in the Supreme Court transcript of Gene's case)

The defence of provocation means that women are not allowed the right to leave a violent situation. (PHIL)

In the absence of evidence of the previous violence inflicted by the accused against his victim, the defence of provocation has been successfully used in domestic murder cases. Taken out of context, the murder is explained as spontaneous and provoked. Many of the families believe that provocation is unfairly used to reduce a charge from murder to manslaughter and to justify low sentences. They believe that it largely relies on a degrading, stereotypical view of women. Men who killed the women they have lived with are too able to convince lawyers, judges and juries that they are the helpless victims of women who have left them or women who have started actively resisting the onslaught of abuse they have endured over the years.

Vicki's ex-de facto argued that he was provoked because she left him and had become involved with someone else. In this case, the magistrate at the committal would not allow the charges to be reduced from murder to manslaughter because she said that there were three different accounts which indicated a prior intention to kill Vicki. The jury at the trial, however, accepted Keogh's defence of provocation and he was found guilty of manslaughter. Her brother Phil said,

> The moral of the story was quite clear: a woman leaves a man at her peril. The man is able to run a defence of provocation very easily. In my sister's case, what was the provocation? Simply that she left a man, that he became depressed? This was murder in my view, not manslaughter.

After the trial Vicki's family urged a review of the law relating to provocation. Phil told the media that the family was devastated by the jury's decision to reduce the conviction to manslaughter. "We feel that the fact that provocation can be pushed to these limits suggests that the law needs to be reviewed", he said. "The verdict of not guilty to murder cheapens my sister's life and cheapens women. It reduces women to chattels and property in a domestic relationship." Vicki's mother told us, "A woman is thought to have made her own bed and must lie in it. Victims have no rights and women have no rights. You don't realise it when you come from a happy home until it happens to you".

Christine's ex-husband was convicted of manslaughter after claiming he had been provoked by her refusal to give up her work as a prostitute and his fear that their children would get AIDS from their mother. In fact, he approved of her work and had been living off her earnings for some years. He shot her when she told him she was leaving him. Carmel told us, "The verdict that she contributed to her own death is simply unacceptable". Christine's sister and friend said, in regard to provocation, "We are concerned that the notion of a 'crime of passion' is encouraging to men who are simply dissatisfied with losing the power in their relationship and that an alarming number of murders occur when women leave or threaten to leave a relationship with a man".

In Gene's case, the Supreme Court judge questioned why her ex-husband was on a charge of manslaughter and not murder. The judge was disturbed by the fact that Schembri had sent Gene a news clipping about another Filipina who had been murdered by her spouse and had written on it: "Good luck to the man as he must have been used as a passport to Australia". He was initially charged with murder, but this was reduced to manslaughter because the DPP believed that he would be successful in raising provocation as a defence. In the committal this provocation was described as her alleged words "I'll do whatever I like", the alleged slapping of his face and what the defence described as her desire for "the fast life, having affairs and living a life independent of him". The prosecution explained to the judge that "the slap to the face, following of course on the conversation which obviously wasn't going in the way in which the accused man had intended that it should, it was on this basis that the Director of Public Prosecutions took the course that he did". Yet there was evidence of premeditation: on the day he killed her, he tricked Gene into thinking that she could see her daughter, but instead had arranged for her daughter to be elsewhere, and had made no preparations for the property settlement hearing the following week.

116

Her friends were angry that the circumstances surrounding the so-called provocation of her (allegedly) slapping him didn't come out — that she had originally left her daughter with him five years earlier because she feared his violence, and that he had subsequently denied her access to her daughter.

In Margaret's case, Jeanette said, the basis of her husband's provocation defence was that she was an alcoholic and that "she had given him nine years of hell and drove him to it". The fact that he had tried to kill her many times, that the police had arrested him for his violence towards her, and that he himself was an alcoholic, was not brought up. His blatantly fabricated assertions about her were never challenged, and the defence of provocation was successful.

In Laurell's case, the trial judge rejected the defence's submissions to treat the girl's death as a "domestic crime or crime of passion". The judge put his own view that it was "more likely to have been committed by a man who knew he was unlikely to retain legal custody of his daughter, and who had killed her rather than lose a custody battle".[10] Nevertheless, in sentencing, the judge reduced the sentence because of what he regarded as provocation. This was overturned on appeal.

At a Bicentennial Family Law Conference in 1989, Mr Justice Vincent, of the Victorian Supreme Court, expressed his concerns about the defence of provocation. He told the conference that he was dismayed that juries readily accept men's violent behaviour towards wives as within the range of ordinary human behaviour. Phil Cleary holds a similar view: "The implications are that women's rights are minimal in a domestic situation and that men are able to object to the most trivial things and that can become a defence, like simply a woman leaving a man...And the man almost has a right to kill her".

Although a majority of the Victorian Law Reform Commission, in their 1991 *Homicide Report*, took the view that the provocation defence generally does not operate in a gender-biased way, the minority views of the commission fit more closely with the experiences of family members. Their views were that provocation:

- "is difficult to express and notoriously difficult to apply and internally inconsistent in allowing some factors to be taken into account, but not others";
- "usually operates in favour of male defendants and against female victims"; and that
- "all deliberate and unjustified killings are murder. The fact that a person killed only after being provoked does not alter the fact that he or she killed intentionally".[11]

The view of the Women's Coalition Against Family Violence is that the provocation defence is applied in a gender-biased way. Men are successful in using provocation where the circumstances do not justify it. The Law Reform Commission concluded that it does not operate in a gender-biased way because the defence is equally successfully used by men and women; however, this assumes that the crimes are comparable.

In reality we know that most killings by women result from long-standing domestic violence against them by the victim, whereas men who kill their partners are usually the perpetrators of previous violence against them. Therefore one would expect many more women to be successful in arguing provocation than men. In fact, until recently the defence of provocation was largely unavailable to women who had killed their male partner, because they killed not "in the heat of the moment" — as is presumed about men who kill women — but after a long history of being abused. For many women their only means of escape is to plan ahead. More recently, some courts have accepted that such a history constitutes provocation.[12]

We would support legislation that would clarify that this is the case. The Women's Coalition Against Family Violence has major concerns about the "battered woman syndrome" which is being raised as a defence where a woman has killed the perpetrator of this abuse.

Researchers Elizabeth Sheely, Julie Stubbs and Julia Tolmie express cogently our reservations. Concluding one of their papers on the battered woman syndrome they say:

> The syndrome as it has been defined and applied, is inherently problematic. Rather than counteracting prejudicial stereotypes of battered women and promoting an unbiased assessment of their circumstances, including their fear of harm, their inability to escape, the unresponsiveness of police, and their lack of other alternatives, it is used to perpetuate existing stereotypes and explain what is wrong with them psychologically. In the short term this might mean more acquittals but at a long-term cost which may well be enormous. It will penalise those defendants who exercise lethal self-help and do not fit within the psychological profile because it both fails to focus on the real issue, the lack of alternatives for battered women, and serves to obscure the fact that existing legal standards of reasonableness fail to incorporate women's experiences.[13]

It is an indictment of the legal system that a woman can be subjected to years of abuse from which the legal system fails to protect her, and yet her abuser successfully uses a legal defence of provocation, merely when a woman acts in ways which are at odds with a man's wishes. As Carmel put it,

> That provocation is used equally by men and women just disguises the issue. Men use provocation for flimsy excuses to murder. She looked at him, she was going to leave etc. Women use it for crimes following years of serious abuse. The way in which women and men can be provoked is genderdefined. Women are not supposed to murder, it's "unladylike".

Self-defence

The legal defence of self-defence was raised by Ann's ex-husband. He claimed that he strangled her because she had stabbed him.

He told the police that he went to her house, knocked, turned to leave, then felt a blow to his shoulder, saw his wife holding a "blood-splattered" knife and he "snapped". There were no witnesses to establish who had caused the injury to him.

Ann's ex-husband was found not guilty of her murder on the grounds of self-defence. The family were not happy with this verdict, and feel that if the prior history of violence had been brought out in court the outcome may have been different. Mary said, "I can't understand it — he did it. He admitted it — there was an obvious motivation and signs of premeditation".

But the motivation and premeditation Mary speaks of didn't come out in court. The years of violence he had subjected her to were not brought up except for an incident witnessed by a neighbour who told the court that he "was aware of ongoing fights, that Mick would threaten Ann and was insanely jealous". Mary told us, "At the trial nothing came out. The ambulance man who attended to Ann was not called. He said Mick's injuries were not life-threatening and there was a slight trickle of blood". Mick told family members, "If I can't have her no-one else can". This didn't come out in court.

There were many contradictions in the court case. A friend of Ann's said, "He got off on the grounds of self-defence, yet his statement was riddled with macho assertions that she didn't hurt him, like 'It didn't hurt me that much', 'I didn't really feel a lot of pain'". A family member told us, "This defence was accepted despite the fact that only one stitch was required. Mick claimed it didn't hurt anyway, he was a black belt in karate. He should not have entered the house anyway, and it was not investigated as to whether he injured himself or whether it was Ann".

More courts — more control

Some family members have commented on the continuing trauma of having to deal with custody applications by the father who had killed the children's mother. Carmel said:

Even if found guilty of murder or manslaughter, men continue to have rights to apply for custody and access to children. The Family Court works on the premise: natural father — natural rights. The process of assessing the applications before the Family Court are particularly brutal. In order to work out whether a murdering father should see his child, the child is ordered to see his or her father so that Family Court counsellors and psychologists can observe their interaction. This process cannot take into account the sheer terror of having to confront someone you had watched kill your mother, knowing that you may have to see him regularly or even be with him forever.

> ...My mother was ordered to take her [Christine's daughter] to the prison for an assessment. She reports her being particularly quiet and scared. I saw her just after she left the prison. She was so shocked and disturbed by the process that she had to have enormous quantities of iced milk to keep her awake. Her eyes rolled back in her head. I saw her mid-morning. He continued making applications for her custody and access to her for six years after he murdered my sister. Her daughter lived in terror of him until he was deported.

If a man is convicted of murdering his wife he has no entitlement to her estate. However, if he is convicted of manslaughter he is entitled to the estate unless she has left a will to the contrary. Since most men who kill their spouses are convicted of manslaughter, this was seen by some families as rewarding their brutality.

CHAPTER SIX

Media complicity in murder

✳

*The reports in the papers of domestic murders are strangely worded.
Whereas other newspaper murder reports talk of horror and waste,
these talk of "devoted family men under financial pressure or who
just reached the end of their tether".[1]*

*Everything the media offers us, whether news or entertainment, is
channelled through people, processes, prejudices, traditions and
pressures of time, resources and competition. What is selected for
exposure (and what is not), how it is edited, constructed and
presented and by whom — all of this is of paramount importance
in structuring and limiting our perceptions.[2]*

The news media insists on its objectivity, claiming that its images
and representations are simply a mirror of our existing reality,
that it is presenting "the facts". As such, the powerful impact of
the media cannot be ignored, both in terms of limiting what
audiences can see and read, and in directing our understanding
of events. The media is influential in shaping public attitudes,
both because it is our source of information about domestic
murders and because of its supposed "objectivity".

Media is one part of the whole system that creates, determines and reinforces attitudes. The media is made up of
journalists, sub-editors and owners who, as individuals, are subject to the same attitudes and values as the broader community.

It is the process of the mass publication of these attitudes and the reception by the audience of them as "authoritative" which does the real damage of distorting the realities of domestic murder.

The media tends to dramatise and fictionalise domestic murder, thus blurring the line between news and drama. The fundamental issues in the reporting of domestic homicide are: the selectivity of the information presented, the willingness of the media to sensationalise the motives or excuses of the murderer and the attempts to find fault with the behaviour of the victims, thereby justifying the killing.

Our discussion of media is largely confined to print media, but the electronic media would be subject to many of the same criticisms.

Media fictions

The reporting of crime has its historical roots firmly embedded in print media. The first newspapers in the English-speaking world reported crime and criminal trials. Interestingly, the media of this century has carried this mantle with even greater zeal — television has unashamedly embraced the drama of crime. Its fictionalisation of crime is often hard to distinguish from its news reporting of it — "infotainment and faction" have blurred many boundaries. The continuing proliferation of "cop" shows is testament to the money to be made from crime. Re-enactments of crimes on news and current affairs programs, police sponsored "catch the crook" segments and the tailing of police by program crews using such dubious titles as "Hard Copy" and "Real Life" further blur the line between news and drama.

The media treats domestic murder, in particular, as entertainment, milking emotion with an emphasis on jealousy, financial ruin and "misguided love". The fictions around domestic violence and murder that are both created and perpetuated in this way are extremely powerful. Because the killer is also the sole living voice of the relationship, it is his views that are published and he has a vested interest in creating sympathy for himself. In some of the cases we looked at it went even further and some journalists embellished facts about the victim.

Families and friends we spoke to were concerned about the distortion of the facts of the case. Some of those we interviewed saw the media as uncritically reinforcing sexual stereotypes that blamed the woman or sympathised with or tried to explain away the killer's actions.

In Vicki's case much of the media concentrated on finding a new twist. There were headlines such as "I loved her", "She betrayed me", "He had a cup of coffee", "It was a blur" and "Threat in pub". In Mirela's case we were enticed by "Man made death weapon at work" (*Sun*).[3] The families were not impressed by the media's claims to responsible journalism. What seemed to be newsworthy was sensationalism, not the depiction of an ordinary woman killed by her partner who wanted to control her.

Newspapers seem to adopt two extremes in their reporting of domestic murder. Often the first reports actually hide the fact that it is a domestic murder behind headlines such as "Woman killed in shooting, man wounded". Once the trials are under way, murder headlines become more florid: "Farm crisis dad kills wife and tots". Such a headline would never appear in the reporting of a police or stranger shooting.

The double standards of the print media are also illustrated in the reporting of the murder of a sixty-year-old woman by her 64-year-old husband. The man murdered his wife by stabbing her in the neck, throat and genitals. He left the knife embedded in her genitals. The *Age* headline read: "Man kills wife after AIDS test jury told". Not only is there an implication that the man contracted the virus from his wife (in fact it was a needle stick injury), the tenor of the whole report is to create sympathy for the man at his distress at being diagnosed HIV positive. This diverted attention from the symbolism of stabbing his wife in the genitals and breasts. His "reasons" were that his wife wouldn't have sex with him or cook for him.[4] In a news report, the Victorian police showed that most non-fatal injuries to women are to the head, breasts and genitals.[5]

A significant feature of almost all the press clippings we looked at from before 1985 was the absence of any emphasis on the relationship within which domestic murders occurred. This is still the case, although to a lesser extent. The headlines often tell us no more than "Man kills woman" or "Woman stabbed by man". The people are often identified by their work or marital status — divorcee, vet, kindergarten assistant, Oakleigh man — but the relationship between the two people is rarely made immediately clear. One story begins: "An eight-year-old girl wounded by shotgun pellets rescued her baby sister from a gunman who killed their mother"; nine paragraphs later the gunman's identity is revealed and we are told the man "chased his estranged wife".[6] This failure to name the relationship between the killer and the dead woman denies the reality of domestic murder. The deaths seem random, with no explanation. The fact that wife-killing is the single largest category of homicide in Victoria is just not apparent from newspaper coverage.

Although crime reporting is a major feature of newspapers, the journalists assigned to court reporting are usually cadets or junior journalists. It may be that their eagerness to produce juicy copy overrides their professional role as reporters of information. The creation of headlines, however, is the responsibility of seasoned sub-editors who can find no excuse in inexperience. The gender of journalists is to an extent also relevant to the way incidents are reported. This has been highlighted in the reporting of the war in Bosnia. This war is the first in which large numbers of women have been major print correspondents. It has been said that in their reports women have focused on the impact of the war on people, rather than reporting on the way the weapons of war are utilised and the viewpoints of military strategists.[7] It would be interesting to see whether this perceptible difference is transferable to the domestic war zone of guns, violence and intimidation.

Filtration through the male cultural sieve not only trivialises the violence and the murder, it often results, too, in the portrayal of the men who murder their wives or children as being quite different from "normal men". These men are portrayed as aberrations — the strangers that we are all taught to fear. The photographs of the men are often so ugly that the impression is created that this is no ordinary man, but someone you could tell by looking was nasty or dangerous.[8] This reinforces the message that it is strangers who are to be feared, not husbands or fathers — although statistically a woman is much more likely to be killed by her husband than by a stranger. The fear of murder by strangers is used in advertising. Soon after the disappearance of schoolgirl Karmein Chan, a Telecom mobile phone advertisement used the image of a young school girl and asked her father if he knew where his daughter was. The model is a young Asian woman in school uniform and, given the virtual absence of Asian people in advertisements except for airlines and holidays, the reference to Karmein Chan's disappearance and murder is obvious. Aside from the exploitation of the murder for commercial gain by the deliberate selection of a young Asian woman and all the images it conjured up at the time, the advertisement reinforces the idea that it is strangers, rather than fathers, that young women have to fear.

It is only relatively recently that domestic killings have been given much space or prominence in the media. A 1979 NSW study of seven years of press cuttings found that killings of strangers for gain received prominent coverage accompanied by exclamations of outrage; domestic homicides, in contrast, were reported as ordinary occurrences and were rarely described with the same sense of outrage or moral panic.[9]

Paradoxically, domestic murders are either sensationalised or virtually ignored. The understatement of domestic murder was commented on by those we interviewed. Jill's sister said, "The media didn't pick up this case because it wasn't really 'spectacular'. It was just another domestic murder. There was a small paragraph on page three of the daily paper". Sue's mother and sister echoed similar sentiments: "There doesn't appear to have been much media. A tiny bit appeared in the *Herald*".

Journalists may argue that they only report what is said in court. Yet it is generally the statements of prosecutors and defence counsel that are reported, often as if they were actual evidence. These statements tend to rely on colourful language and dramatic presentation, and contain the most fantastic possibilities. In this way newspapers become tools of lawyers in putting forward the defendant's perspective rather than being reporters of the evidence. As Kay said, "The media just make headlines — and you just have to wear it. The media took it from transcripts — they just took passages — it wasn't in context so they could give a particular idea which wasn't true".

What emerges from the media, then, is a distorted view of domestic murder. This comes about because of the silencing of the murdered woman's voice. Then there is the omission of facts like the nature of the relationship between the woman and man. This is compounded by the media's treatment of murder as entertainment.

Media policespeak

Police rounds reporters in effect become de facto reporters of the police version of events.[10] In Victoria, the police units of the *Age* and the *Sun* were located two buildings down from the eighteen-storey police headquarters. Journalists who criticise the police don't get to have lunch with them and so don't get information and stories from them. As these very stories are what the journalists are there to cover, they are faced with a dilemma. All too often these journalists report exclusively the police version of events rather than doing any independent or investigative work. It is established police practice to give "good" stories selectively to those journalists who print what police want printed. The publication of police attitudes in the guise of journalists' stories further gives these attitudes an appearance of objectivity

and authority, and the act of publication is a widespread reinforcement of the view of the male police culture.

The consequences of the relationship between the media
and police created problems for the families. The media frequently knew and publicised deaths before family members were
informed. In one case the media published tape recordings of
Chris's children made just before they were murdered. The first
the family knew of these tapes was reading part of their transcript in the press. Chris told us, "I saw bits of it in the
newspaper. I rang the police — I was outraged. Police said I
could hear it if I wanted to, but they didn't recommend it. The
kids' voices are on it. I still haven't".

Jill's sister Judy told us, "The night of the murder, there
was a newsflash broadcast on television. The house was easily
recognised. This was how one of my sisters learned of Jill's murder".

SEVEN WAYS MEN ARE NOT RESPONSIBLE FOR THE MURDERS

The most prominent feature of all the clippings we saw reporting these murders was the lengths to which some journalists
went to shift the blame and responsibility for the murder away
from the man who killed and onto some other phenomenon or
onto the woman herself. In failing to acknowledge that it is men
who are murdering women and children, the media is firmly
implicated in one of the most dangerous of cover-ups.

1. What killed her?

"Love pulls the trigger" (Sunday Press 5 March 1989)

The fact that a man has killed a woman is often obscured by
shifting the blame to something else. What killed her, we are

told, was a knife, despair, a domestic dispute, marriage difficulties, a bottle, or even love. If the responsibility for the murder is not shifted to something else, it is placed firmly within the relationship which implicates the woman, as partly responsible for her own death.

In the headline "Despair prompts killing" (*Sun*),[11] we see the focus shifted away from the man. This time "despair" stabbed, bashed and burnt two young children to death. The report focuses on the perpetrator as a victim, humiliated when his ex-wife called the police in front of her mother. Much was made of the cultural significance of the shame of this. There was also mention in the media of his having money in the failed Pyramid Building Society, although this was not raised as an explanation at the trial. It is almost as though the murder happened "accidentally" and is a tragedy for which nobody is responsible. Chris said, "He had money in Pyramid so of course the press made something of it".

In Gene's case one headline was "Dream marriage ends in death" (*Age*).[12] Another headline, "Death on a Sunday morning" (*Age*),[13] has a peaceful ring about it, in contrast to the reality of Gene's being strangled to death. It begins: "Jonathan Green reports on the history of a troubled marriage". The neutral word "troubled" is used often. There are many references throughout the report to "trouble" arising; "After five months of marriage Charlie sensed trouble". The reporter then lists the failings and omissions of both partners, conveying the belief that the responsibility for the killing could not easily be placed.

The headline, "The family that death wouldn't let go" (*Sun*)[14] refers to a man's killing of his wife and children. Using terms like "family murders" and "family tragedies" conceals the fact that a man has brutally killed three people. Not only is the fact that a man has murdered his wife and children obscured, there is almost a suggestion of complicity by all involved. The fact that a crime has occurred is passed over — they just died. Indeed there is no real offender, for he too is seen to be a victim.

"Love pulls the trigger" is the headline of a feature article on the death of Christine Boyce. Christine was shot dead the day before a Family Court custody contest. Kevin Crowe, Christine's former husband, had carried the .22 rifle in his car for a year and had earlier said he might shoot Christine in the breast and disfigure her so that she could not continue working in the sex industry.

2. He is a victim too

"Day of death; dad dies after shooting spree" (*Sun* 14 September 1989)

The humanising impact of the phrase "family tragedy" and representations of "family murder" as involving only victims and no offender is a recurring theme in press reports. Often such reports find explanation for the murder primarily in social stress factors such as poverty, unemployment, drinking and isolation. While these issues urgently require action, resources and structural change, it is clear that they don't explain the gender basis and bias of domestic murders.

As well as being portrayed as victims of these social stress factors men are also portrayed as hapless victims of their own actions, or they are thwarted by love, or manipulated by their female partner. In each instance the individual man is not seen to be totally responsible for killing his partner, children, or himself. "Day of death; dad dies after shooting spree" does not give the impression that this man shot and killed his wife and eight-month-old baby with a .22 rifle.

The trial of Dennis McBride, who shot and killed his twelve-year-old daughter, was reported in these terms: "[he] had punished himself more than a judge ever could, the man's counsel said yesterday...[he] was still grieving over the loss of his daughter" (*Age*).[15] The use of the word "loss" disguises the fact that he was the one who murdered Laurell. The report chooses to highlight the father's emotional state, not his actions and the suggestion that he couldn't really be held fully responsible sends the media looking for who or what is. The report goes on to blame Laurell's mother by implication: "Mrs McBride had agreed that McBride, who had a gun at the meeting, could have Laurell live with him". The word "agreed" does not seem an appropriate description of Mrs McBride's response to her husband's having a gun, or his threats to kill her and her children if she didn't comply.

The article further suggests that because of his "moral" worthiness as a "hard working man who had provided for his family", McBride should be excused for his crime. Mrs McBride is also seen to bear some responsibility and blame as an "older woman", for whom McBride gave up his position in the police force: "McBride had married Kay when he was almost nineteen and she was twenty-five, having left the police force to be with her and there had been problems in the marriage".[16]

The suggestion is that she was a destabilising influence on him and, in accordance with popular stereotypes, the older woman corrupting a man. In this case the perpetrator becomes the victim. Finally, "problems in their marriage" is used to obscure the years of extreme abuse that the family endured at the hands of McBride and which culminated in him shooting and killing their daughter.

The reports of Gene's death told a story which portrayed Charlie Shembri as a hapless victim. A *Sun* report said:

> He wanted a reconciliation, had even had plastic surgery soon after their separation to improve his chances with a wife ten years his junior but Gene remained resolute. Charlie was fed up. If necessary he would go back to the Family Court. That would be, he knew, an expensive process. Now unemployed with a back problem Charlie could ill afford the expense. The stress of joblessness and his anxieties over Gene and his daughter…His beloved Gene took everything leaving him with Alice and a fridge.[17]

The *Age* reported that "Gene was motionless in her blue tracksuit, her long hair spread out on the living room floor. He said he bent down and picked up her hand. Her nails were long and neat and painted red".[18]

From friends we heard a different version. Gene had left Charlie several times in the first two years of the marriage due to his verbal and physical violence. When she did separate from him he constantly harassed her and used their daughter as a means of hurting her. She was forced to leave Alice with him because he threatened to kill her if she tried to take her daughter with her.

Initially, the coverage reflected Schembri's contention that Gene had used him as a passport.[19] The Collective of Filipinas for Empowerment and Development, a group which grew out of the Filipina involvement in Gene's case, wrote to newspapers protesting at the sexist and racist coverage. This changed the representation of Schembri a little. He was later portrayed as a naive man who had been foolish enough to believe that he could buy love. Indeed three of his friends who married Filipina women for their "submissive character and virtue" were now all divorced and "had lost considerable amounts of money and property through the marriages" (*Sun*).[20] Gene "lost" her life. The effect of the change in media coverage was to marginalise Schembri and treat the case as an isolated personal tragedy: "Dream marriage ends in death: a romance made in the Philippines led to tragedy" (*Age*).[21] A feature in the *Sunday Age*[22] juxtaposes Gene's marriage with another Filipina–Australian marriage. It is implied that in spite of cultural differences, the norm is for these marriages to work, as opposed to the oddity of Gene's death at Schembri's hands. The implication is that Gene and especially Schembri were just unlucky, and that Schembri perhaps wasn't culturally sensitive enough. Race and gender issues in domestic violence and murder were far from being addressed.

Inaccuracies in facts and blaming the victim remained a focus in the reports, for example Gene's alleged desire for the "night life" and "life in the fast lane". We even read of "Gene's long fingernails leaving scratches on Schembri's left arm and chest. She fell. Charlie kept his grip until she was dead" (*Sun*).[23] All later articles also uncritically reflected Schembri's disapproval of Gene's insistence on sending some of her own money home to her family.

A strong identification with and sympathy for the killer were evident in the report of a murder where a man shot and killed his wife, three daughters and then himself. It is headlined "Bill snap on family man" (*Sun*).[24] The report predominantly focuses on his stresses over money. He is described as a "devoted family man...a non-drinking hard worker". His only crimes, we are told, were "his pride and he would buy items to keep up with the Joneses".

In the reporting of one murder a headline reads: "——— tells court he had considered suicide" (*Northern Star*).[25] The rest of the text presents a substantial part of his statement from the dock designed to engender sympathy for him. In the murder of Margaret the headline reads "Taxi man charged with wife murder had life in hell, court told" (*Sun*)[26] The story goes on that Margaret had a fractured skull and broken neck from being repeatedly punched in the head while she was in the bath, before her body was placed in a briquette bag and driven around in the boot of his taxi. The "life in hell" consisted of allegations of drinking and affairs. Margaret's daughter told us about the other side of the life in hell. This was not the first time he'd tried to kill her; both children and Margaret lived in constant fear of his violence.

3. He lost control

"Cheque man snapped" (*Sun* 15 June 1990)

Another insidious means of denying the perpetrator's responsibility for his actions is to acknowledge that he did perform the violence but that he did so because he "lost control" or "snapped". Men claim they lose control of their emotions, when in fact they have claimed final control over the lives they have ended.

In Ann's case the headline "Cheque man snapped", referred to the maintenance cheque her husband alleged he had been delivering to her prior to killing her. Other men's killings were similarly explained. In "Cat row killing" (*Sun*)[27] Peter Taylor "lost control" and murdered his wife after she yelled at him for knocking over a cat bowl. Thomas Dodd also snapped. He'd gone with a knife into the bathroom while his wife was running a bath "hoping to touch her so that she would melt into his arms". Instead he "snapped...and slashed the knife across her throat four times" (*Sun*).[28] Charles Schembri said that after Gene swore at him and slapped his face he "couldn't let go, I couldn't let go".

The assumption seems to be that some men are governed by uncontrollable urges to inflict violence on women and they cannot be held accountable for this. This myth is extremely pervasive in our society and one which the media readily upholds. The real question is why is it that it is primarily men who "lose control", and why is it that they lose control primarily against the women with whom they live, or have lived?

4. He was a nice bloke

As is often reported by victims of domestic violence people cannot believe "he did it" because he is a "nice ordinary bloke". In the article headed "Farm crisis dad kills wife, tots" (*Sun*),[29] it was reported that "A family of four killed in a murder–suicide at a farm house had been suffering financial hardship". The story goes on to say, "Shocked friends yesterday told of the family's money worries…'We are very shocked. No one could believe it could happen to such a nice bloke.'" He emerges as a person of complex emotions deserving of sympathy. The choice of language in this headline determines how we receive and interpret the information. The report is openly sympathetic to the man and effectively renders the murder of the woman and her children a secondary issue. In fact, she is absent from the picture. We are never told of the stresses imposed on her, whether there was previous violence, or how his stress can legitimise the murder of three other people.

Under the headline "Son killed for love", where a man shot his wife and eight month old baby a week after they had separated, we are told: "He wasn't a murderer, says father…he was a good husband, kind hearted and a good mate…he must have been hurting so much inside" (*Sun*).[30] The comment illustrates a community view that murderers can not be ordinary men, they are monsters. The story goes on under the heading "Heartbroken" that a previous girlfriend "spat the dummy" by leaving him and putting the baby up for adoption.

In a story headed "A doctor, his wife and four-year-old daughter found shot dead." (*Sun*),[31] the media concentrates on the man, a local doctor — a "quiet", "warm" and "wonderful man with a keen sense of community duty". The report goes on to describe the murder suicide as a "tragedy", and refers to him as the "first victim". The young child's murder is then briefly referred to and finally the "wife's". While he is named both in terms of his profession and his characteristics all that is revealed of the murdered woman is her age, attractiveness and racial background. She has no identity other than as his wife. The fact that she was a victim of his violence is lost in the proposition that they were all victims.

5. He did it for love

"Kill case man's love plea" (*Sun* 11 February 1989)

Media reports of domestic killings often uncritically accept the notion that men are violent and abusive towards women as a demonstration of their love for them. The media has revelled in sensationalist headlines such as "Love pulls the trigger", with text like "Around nine p.m. her second husband…shot dead the woman he worshipped". Throughout this report there are references to his having a "loving character" and being "a softly spoken person who couldn't raise his voice to her".

In Gene's case the media reported that he was "besotted, enjoying true happiness for the first time since his failed first marriage and was keen to accommodate his wife".[32] Schembri was portrayed as a naive man who had been foolish enough to believe that he could buy love and killed for love. In court, his plea of provocation was largely based on her lifestyle, her swearing at him and her using him to get to Australia; however the media took it upon itself to narrow down the scenario to a love tragedy. We are told under the heading "Jealous killer gets eight years" that a "man who went overseas looking for love was jailed yesterday for killing his beautiful wife. [His] dream marriage…turned to a nightmare and he strangled her in a fit of jealousy" (*Sun*).[33]

One of the reports of Vicki's case was under the heading "Kill case man's love plea". There is little critical analysis of what it could possibly mean to kill for love. It seems that men who have bludgeoned their partners to death are being praised for their devotion. "His love for Paula was so strong he did not want anyone else to love them." (*Sun*)[34]

"Crimes of passion" is the headline of a feature article that appeared in the *Age*[35,] and is a good example of the way the media trivialises violence against women. The very title serves to disguise both the violence and the criminal nature of such acts. An assumption is made that domestic murders arise from the couple's individual circumstances, the strains and problems of cohabitation, the stress and frustration of sexual "passion". Yet, if domestic murders are "caused" by these purely personal factors, why is there a gross difference between men who kill and women who kill? Either partner in a marriage or relationship can feel stress and frustration, yet it is almost invariably men who resort to murder.

136

6. He didn't mean it — he was mad

"Sick man shot wife six times" (*Sun* 22 June 1990)

Domestic killers are often portrayed as madmen or psychopaths. Their killing of a wife or children is regarded as just another aspect of their madness, and the media seems quick to accept such a simplistic explanation. There is also a reverence for the word of the expert. In their attempts to prove the aberrant nature of these killers, journalists and the court seek out the views of the "expert" as the final authority on the question of someone's sanity. The expert criminologist or psychiatrist is portrayed in the media as concerned simply with establishing the truth, while the family's story contains ambiguity showing a concern for feelings rather than facts. The reader is encouraged to accept the truth of the expert's viewpoint through the use of verbs such as "stated", "reported" or "disclosed" which all have a definite and factual ring about them. In contrast, when families are interviewed their statements are referred to as "claims" or "assertions".

One family member described this imbalance: "I knew him for ten years and yet my observations regarding his sanity were ignored. Yet an interview conducted for six hours by the psychiatrist established his insanity beyond a doubt".

In Mirela's case the media focused on a combination of her behaviour (he blamed her for the death of his mother/she "insisted" on his release) and his madness. The headline was "Wife insisted on husband's release" (*Sun*)[36] and we were told, "A woman allegedly slain by her paranoid husband had won his release from psychiatric care, a court heard yesterday". In later reports a lead paragraph read "the death of a Northcote woman might have been avoided if she had left her schizophrenic husband in hospital, a court heard yesterday" (*Sun*).[37]

The article then largely relied on the view of an expert: The "psychiatrist described the case as a tragic crime by a psychotic patient". The defence asked the doctor about a relative's claims that his behaviour was a sham to set himself up for an insanity defence. The doctor replied, "It is hard to know. I did not get the impression he was manipulating or covering up in any way. No signs pointed to that". It is a pity that the doctor didn't comment on the years of violence Mirela's husband inflicted on her as some explanation of his behaviour. Helen, Mirela's friend, remarked, "Perhaps he is at the far end of the spectrum but then you wonder where the whole definition of psychiatric illness begins".

7. She provoked it

"Two lovers tell — wife aimed to leave — friend" (*Sun* 3 November 1990)

"Affairs a shock: dad" (*Sun* 8 November 1990)

"She had me fooled: lover" (*Sun* 9 November 1990)

It has been said that "the media provides us with models of behaviour aimed at shaping us into socially acceptable females, and with cautionary tales warns us of the unpleasant results of ignoring their advice."[38] The continued stereotyping of women serves to place the blame on the woman: the presumption is that for deviating from what is expected of her as a woman she has somehow brought about her own violent death. It seems men are eminently provocable, and women may be punished for leaving them, or for real or imagined expressions of sexuality. The media reinforces what is normal and acceptable within society as well as what is mad and bad.

Women who are murdered, obviously, can't speak out on their own behalf. We don't get to hear from them or hear about their understanding of what was happening in their relationships. And, strikingly, the media rarely makes any attempt to portray the murder from the perspective of the murdered woman or to include any previous history of domestic violence.

Often, as we have seen, this history is not brought up in court and prior to trial it would be prejudicial for journalists to mention it. Nevertheless, it was a strong view of families and friends we spoke to that "her story" should be told. Until quite recently journalists were not interested in pursuing this perspective. Many of the families and friends believed that journalists had already passed their own judgement on such cases.

Some reports display an obsessive preoccupation with the behaviour and characteristics of the murdered woman. In the headlines quoted above, the man's crime was secondary to concerns about the behaviour of the woman. Throughout each of the reports that followed from these headlines the reader is drawn into a moral assessment of the woman victim.

A report headlined "Two lovers tell" (*Sun*)[39] begins: "An attractive Cockatoo woman planned to leave her husband for the last of her three lovers just before she died". The attached photograph serves to reinforce the idea that being conventionally attractive is synonymous with promiscuity. In an earlier report a picture of the woman is captioned "Attractive Blonde";[40] her request that her husband use condoms was also considered newsworthy.[41] Yet another headline, "Wife had 3 lovers", is followed by the lead paragraph, "A murdered woman had a succession of extra-marital affairs according to gossip by local Country Fire Authority Brigade members, a court heard yesterday".[42] Under the headline "Court told of fire victim's lovers", the main body of the story shows that the woman died from head injuries.[43]

Evidence of rumours of the woman's affairs was reported throughout the trial, but it was not until her husband was found guilty of murder that the media reported that his shotgun and prized CFA badges and a coin collection were removed from the house before the murder and fire and placed in his truck. Another report begins with, "The parents of an allegedly murdered woman were surprised and shocked to discover she had extra-marital affairs".[44] We do not read, "His parents were shocked and horrified that he chose to murder the woman he loved and had married".

Many families we interviewed felt frustrated and angry about this type of reporting. Anne, Teresa's sister, remarked, "Parts of the media — I thought, 'What an excuse — they are trying to justify it'. The media played on the rumours of her having an affair".

In our society a prostitute is held up as the archetypal bad woman. The endorsement of this prejudice against women who work in the sex industry is apparent in a report that referred to "A man who shot his wife after becoming distressed when she repeatedly refused to give up her job as a prostitute" (*Sun*).[45] It is suggested that the woman, by virtue of her profession, is in some way responsible for the "punishment" meted out to her, and even perhaps that her husband had a right to kill her since she was working in the sex industry.

The headlines and reporting of domestic murder can reinforce the pressure for women to be seen as good mothers even at the point of murder. One article was headlined "Mum slain as girls watched" (*Sun*).[46] The outrage is expressed not because a man has killed his wife, but because he has done so in front of their young children, and in doing so has deprived them of a mother. In another report the dead woman was portrayed as weak, lacking in the qualities required of a protective mother and trying to "cower" from him in the child's lap.

The press often reports hearsay information in relation to murdered women which implies that the woman is responsible for her own murder; for example "Witnesses gave evidence that Hamilton [the murdered woman] had an obsession with knives, that she was aggressive and would threaten people" (*Ballarat Courier*).[47] Ann's sister said that she herself was portrayed in the media as "a raving loony" because she shouted at Mick.

Good woman, bad woman, or crazy woman; all these representations shift the focus of responsibility for the killing from the perpetrator to the victim. They maintain the myth that in some way women deserve or are responsible for their violent deaths, that men are victims of women and that women do not have a right to live independently without retribution from men.

The media is perhaps the most influential moulder of community opinion and attitude. It must acknowledge the perspective that it takes and the responsibility it has to the community as well as to its shareholders. Unless it does this it will continue to peddle fictions that are potentially fatal.

Remembering

✳

This book exposes the hidden level of violence inflicted on women and children who have been killed by the men in their lives. It exposes the complicity of the legal system in maintaining this violence. It exposes the complicity of the wider community, whose attitudes continue to condone male violence against women and children and deny the responsibility of the offender. It demonstrates that the entire community must take action if the violence and murders are to be prevented. It argues that change which addresses the social and economic inequality of women and children in relation to men in our society must occur in order to end the violence and killings.

Remembering Paul and Lisa

Little Paul who was eight years and eight months old when he was brutally slain will always be remembered as such a happy, cheeky and jolly little chap who would always make you laugh or smile with his antics even if you were feeling down in the dumps. He had so much energy, that it would make you tired just to watch him. He was so outgoing and friendly. His deafness posed no problem for him in making new friends. He didn't need language to communicate. His smile and cheerfulness were enough for people to like him and want to be his friend.

He had to struggle from the moment he was conceived. I contracted malaria, hepatitis and rubella when I was pregnant. The birth was brought on early because he was not receiving enough nutrition and eventually he was born by caesarean section because of his weak heart. He had a heart condition then for the rest of his life, he was in and out of hospital for a variety of problems. He was diagnosed at thirteen months as being severely to profoundly deaf, and if that was not enough, he had to deal with a bastard of a father who would beat him from the age of two years.

Paul broke all the odds and ignored all of his problems and turned into a beautiful little loving boy. He made an impact on everyone he met. Children he met during his short life will always remember him because he stood out in a crowd and he made everyone happy — everyone except his father. His father wanted another male child to replace Paul because of his disability. He saw him as a failure. He never saw him as a beautiful little boy who gave so much but just happened to be deaf. Paul was just so special, he will be remembered by so many people.

Little Lisa was just five years and eight months old when she was murdered. She was a pretty little girl who loved pretty and beautiful things. She was also outgoing and had lots of confidence without being precocious.

She was a delightful, loving, gentle and soft little girl who always had a smile or hug for everyone. She was so proud and protective of her brother and would help him out whenever she could such as by acting as an interpreter.

Paul required a lot of time and attention and his activities took first place in the household. Lisa never complained about this situation once. She was happy to just go along for the ride or to remain quietly in the background. If it made Paul happy, then she was happy.

She had a beautiful, loving, caring, sharing and kind nature. She loved to do things for people. She always wanted to please people and make them happy. She loved to share her things and she had lots of school friends. Everyone wanted to be her friend.

She was a high achiever and very athletic and would have been very successful in whatever area she chose. She loved her dancing and she loved the pretty costumes she wore for the concerts. She loved pretty clothes and she loved to change her hairstyles every day to make herself pretty.

She was my little companion. I will always remember the little chats we would have. She seemed so mature for her years. She was an angel who was sent to me for too short a time.

Were Paul and Lisa both too good for this world?

CHRIS

Remembering Teresa

We heard the door slam,
and you were gone.
The rain like tears in our eyes
signify our pain that will never die.
We long to touch your smile
but in the nights that
slowly close in.

In our field that's so lonely
touching heat we pretend we
still hold you.

We're in too deep over you, we can't believe you're gone.
Wherever you go we'll be with you.
Whenever we need some one,
we lay our hearts on you.
'Cause after the fire,
after all the rain
you'll always be the flame.

ANNE

Remembering Jill

Jill was a third generation woman in my family who was a victim of domestic violence. As a child, she repeatedly witnessed the physical, emotional and verbal abuse of her mother. She saw, as well as heard about, the physical and emotional abuse of her grandmother. She married a man who physically, emotionally and verbally abused her. Domestic violence played a big part in her life.

Despite this fact, however, she was an outgoing, caring and loving woman. Everybody loved Jill — she was an irrepressible, free spirited, fun loving person.

She was unhappy in her marriage, and decided to leave her husband. The price she paid for that decision was her life.

As a surviving family member, I invite society to share my, and my family's pain. I also invite society to share the blame and guilt for my sisters death. Because it is we, as a society, that allowed her killer to believe that he had "ownership rights" over his wife. Even to the point of murdering her — because he lost control of his "possession". My pain and anger are as strong today, as when Jill was murdered, ten years ago. My sister did not deserve to die.

What are we, as a society to do to ensure that no women and children lose their lives at the hand of the man who supposedly "loves" them?

The majority of us believe that domestic violence and domestic murders are none of our business. We are all responsible for the abuse, pain and deaths, and it's high time we faced up to our responsibilities and did something about it.

JUDY

145

Remembering Ann

Ann
Born 1954
Died 1989

My beautiful sister Ann.

If only there were more good people like you. The tears still flow so deeply and the pain keeps hurting. The sadness that surrounds me watching all who love you so much fading away in their own pain, keeps reminding me of how empty and helpless we all feel. My only wish for you now is that you may now finally find some peace.

I will always be your loving sister even after death.

MARY

＊

We also remember Mirela, Vicki, Margaret, Sue, Gene, Laurell, Christine and all of the women and children who have been killed by the men in their lives.

Notes

✳

Introduction

1. This figure is derived from calculations we made after examining the Victorian police homicide squad's homicide register 1985–90. The calculations take account of murder–suicides: murders of women which are recorded by police as suspicious deaths but, due to inadequate evidence, are not pursued. It also includes suicides where a brief investigation takes place and the police consider the circumstances suspicious, but go no further. Statistics we have looked at also vary according to the definition applied by the agency which compiles them. We have chosen a broad definition of domestic homicide which includes all forms of intimate relationships and family relationships.

2. Law Reform Commission of Victoria, *Discussion Paper No. 13: Homicide*, 1988, pp. 11–13.

3. Law Reform Commission of Victoria, *Report No. 40: Homicide*, 1991, p. 4, Note 6.

4. Queensland Domestic Violence Task Force, *Beyond These Walls*, Brisbane, 1988, p. 15.

5. National Committee on Violence, *Violence: Directions for Australia*, Australian Institute of Criminology, Canberra, 1990, p. 33.

6. Women's Policy Co-ordination Unit, Department of Premier and Cabinet, *Criminal Assault in the Home: Social and Legal Responses to Domestic Violence*, Melbourne, 1985, p. 12.

7. Elliott and Shanahan research conducted for the Office of the Status of Women, Department of the Prime Minister and Cabinet, 1988: "Summary of background research for the development of a campaign against domestic violence", p. 148; J. Scutt; *Even in the Best Of Homes: Violence in the Family*, Penguin, Ringwood, 1983.

Chapter 1 — Power & control through violence

1. Jocelynne Scutt, quoted in the National Committee on Violence, *Violence: Directions for Australia*, AIC, Canberra, 1990, p. 101.

2. Public Policy Research Centre, *Domestic Violence Attitude Survey*, conducted for the Office of the Status of Women, Department of the Prime Minister and Cabinet, 1988.

3. There has been research which shows that the incidence of sexual, emotional and physical abuse of children is high in families where the mother is subjected to violence: see C. Goddard, "Child Abuse: A Hospital Study", Honours Thesis (Social Work), Monash University, 1981.

Chapter 2 — Permission to kill

1. *Domestic Violence Attitude Survey*, Executive Summary, p. 23.

2. *Domestic Violence Attitude Survey*, p. 30.

3. G. Wilt et al., *Domestic Violence and the Police: Studies in Detroit and Kansas City 1977*, cited in *Homicide Report No. 40*, p. 23.

4. *Domestic Violence Attitude Survey* p. 27.

5. J. Mugford, S. Mugford and P. Easteal, "Social justice, public perceptions and spouse assault", *Social Justice* , vol. 16 no. 3, 1989, p. 108.

6. *Beyond These Walls*, report of the Queensland Domestic Violence Task Force to the Minister for Family Services and Welfare Housing. Brisbane 1988 p. 13.

7. Elliott & Shanahan.

8. Mugford, Mugford & Esteal, p. 106.

9. Elliott & Shanahan, p. 111.

10. Elliott & Shanahan, p. 111.

11. S. Hatty and J. Sutton, "Policing violence against women", in National Conference on Domestic Violence, 2 vols, S. Hatty(ed.), AIC, Canberra, 1986; Mugford, Mugford & Esteal, pp. 103–20 ; J. Crancher, S. Egger & W. Bacon, "Battered women", in *Issues in Criminal Justice Administration*, M. Findlay, S. Egger and J. Sutton (eds), Allen & Unwin, Sydney, 1983; E. Starke, A. Flitcraft and W. Frazier, "Medicine and patriarchal violence: the social construction of a private event", *International Journal of Health Services*, vol. 9 no. 3, 1979; Centre Against Sexual Assault, *A Pastoral Report to the Churches on Sexual Violence against Women and Children of the Church Community (Project Anna)*, Melbourne, 1990.

12. Elliott & Shanahan, p. 163.

13. Elliott & Shanahan, p. 164.

14. P. Innes, "Women and the Law, women lose their awe of the Law", *Age* 16 January 1993.

15. L. Porter, *Sunday Age*, 1993.

16. Real Rape Law Coalition, 1991, *No Real Justice*, cited in W. Larcombe, "Sexual assault phone-in, no real justice", in Federation of Community Legal Centres, *Hearsay Newsletter*, issue 31, August–September 1991, p. 4.
17. L. Porter, *Sunday Age*, "Who judges the judges", 1993.
18. P. Hughes, "Action urged over judges' rape comments", *Age* 13 January 1993.
19. Elliott & Shanahan, p. 162.
20. Elliott & Shanahan, p. 125.

Chapter 3 — Leaving

1. A. Wallace, *Homicide: The Social Reality*, New South Wales Bureau of Crime Statistics and Research, Sydney, 1986, p 103.
2. R. Western, "Changes in household income circumstances", in *Setting Up: Property and Income Distribution on Divorce in Australia*, P. McDonald (ed.), Australian Institute of Family Studies & Prentice Hall, 1989, chapter 6.
3. Scutt, *Even In the Best of Homes*.
4. For more detailed analysis of women's economic position in society, see L. Beaton, *The Victorian Woman's Workly: Doing Double Time*, Victorian Women's Trust, Melbourne, 1991; C. O'Donnell and P. Hall, *Getting Equal: Labour Market Regulation and Women's Work*, Allen & Unwin, Sydney, 1988; B. Caine, "Equal pay, a family wage, or both', in *Crossing Boundaries*, E. Groth (ed.), Allen & Unwin, Sydney, 1988.
5. *Women in Australia*, Australian Bureau of Statistics, Canberra, 1993, p. 157.
6. *Women in Australia*, p. 157.
7. Marilyn Waring, *Counting for Nothing: What Men Value and What Women are Worth*, Allen & Unwin, Sydney, 1990; *Women and Work*, Australian Bureau of Statistics, 1993.
8. *Women and Award Restructuring: Introduction*, Department of Labour, Women's Employment Branch, Victoria, 1989, p. 13.
9. *Women in Australia*, p. 179.
10. *Women in Australia*, chapter 5.
11. *Women in Australia*, p 125.
12. National Women's Consultative Council, *Women In The Home*, Melbourne, 1988.
13. *Women and Award Restructuring*, p. 5.
14. A. Curthoys, "The sexual division of labour: theoretical arguments', in *Australian Women; New Feminist Perspectives*, N. Grieve and A. Burns (eds), Oxford University Press, Melbourne, 1991; J. Martin, "Non-English-speaking women in Australia", in *Gender at Work*, A. Game and R Pringle(eds), Allen & Unwin, Sydney, 1983.

15. Martin in Game & Pringle, pp. 233–47.

16. *Women in Australia*, p124. See also J. Martin in Game & Pringle, p. 240.

17 *Women in Australia*, p. 136.

18. *Poverty, Poor Choices,* Brotherhood of St Laurence, Victoria, 1990; see also P. Saunders and G. Matheson, "Sole parent families in Australia", monograph no. 19, University of NSW, Kensington, September 1990, quoted in *Services into the 1990s and Beyond,* Women's Services Coalition, Melbourne, 1991, p. 19.

19. G. Foard, *Housing Poverty in the Private Rental Market,* Tenants' Union of Victoria, 1989, p. 14.

20. Ministry of Housing and Construction Victoria, *Rental Report,* March quarter 1989, p. 2.

21. *Cos It's Your Income You Won't Complain: Social Security Phone-in Report,* Federation of Community Legal Centres et al., 1991.

22. *Do You Feel Safe Here: A Study of Young Women's Experiences in Youth Housing and Refuges,* Young Women's Housing Collective, Melbourne, 1991.

23. B. Burdekin, *Our Homeless Children,* report of the National Inquiry into Homeless Children, Human Rights and Equal Opportunity Commission, Canberra, 1989; C. Hirst, *Forced Exit: A Profile of the Young Homeless in Inner Urban Melbourne,* report of the Salvation Army Youth Homelessness Policy Development Project, Salvation Army Crossroads Youth Project, Melbourne, 1989.

24. *Sunday Age,* 20 March 1994, p. 1.

25. Fitzroy/Collingwood Accommodation Service statistics.

26. *Rooming Houses And The People Who Live In Them,* report from the Ministry of Consumer Affairs and Rooming House Tenants' Association; Victoria, September 1992.

27. Youth Homelessness Working Group, *A Place For Young People: A Community Review of the Federal and Victorian Governments' Responses to Homeless Young People,* VCOSS paper no.4, September 1990, p. 21.

28. *Australia's One Parent Families,* Australian Bureau of Statistics, catalogue no. 2511.0.

29. *Tenant Self-advocacy Phone-in Report,* Council for Single Mothers and their Children, Melbourne, 1992.

30. *Women in Australia*, p. 214.

31. *Poverty: Poor Choices* , p. 5.

32. *Poverty: Poor Choices* , p. 5.

33. G. Foard, p.23.

34. P. Kennedy and M. Paul, *No Place for Women: Women and Housing,* Women in Supportive Housing, Melbourne, 1988.

35. V. Milligan, quoted in Kennedy & Paul, p. 37.

36. Second National Women's Conference, Australia, 1987.

Chapter 4 — Before the killing — the legal system

1. J. Hanmer, J. Radford and E. Stanko (eds), *Women, Policing and Male Violence*, Routledge, London, 1989, p.18.

2. K. J. Ferraro, "The legal response to woman battering in the United States", in Hanmer, Radford & Stanko, p. 182.

3. Ferraro in Hanmer, Radford & Stanko.

4. *Sexual Assault Victims and the Police*, Police Complaints Authority Victoria discussion paper, April 1988, p. 17.

5. H. Van Moorst, *The Attitude of Professionals*, Footscray Institute of Technology.

6. J. McCulloch and L. Schetzer, *Brute Force: The Need for Affirmative Action in the Victorian Police Force*, The Federation of Community Legal Centres, Melbourne, 1993, p. 1.

7. E. Stanko, "Missing the mark?: police battering", in Hanmer, Radford & Stanko, p. 47.

8. S. Hatty, *Male Violence and the Police, an Australian Experience*, School of Social Work, University of NSW, 1988, p. 179.

9. Hatty, *Male Violence*.

10. J. Hunt, "The development of rapport through the negotiation of gender in field work among police', *Human Organisation*, vol. 43 no. 4, pp. 293–6.

11. S. Hatty, "Policing and male violence in Australia', in Hanmer, Radford & Stanko, p. 106.

12. O. J. Zoomer, "Policing woman beating in the Netherlands', in Hanmer, Radford & Stanko, p. 143.

13. *Police Life*, August 1992.

14. R. Wearing, "Monitoring the impact of the *Crimes (Family Violence) Act 1987*", LaTrobe University, Melbourne, 1992, quoted in McCulloch & Schetzer, .p. 12.

15. *Victoria Police Manual*, 1.3.3: Family Violence 1–26.

16. *Victoria Police Manual*, 1.3.3. Family Violence 1–27.

17. *Victoria Police Manual*, 1.3.3; *Firearms Act 1958* s. 3.

18. Renata Alexander (family law solicitor, Legal Aid Commission of Victoria), "Submission to Social Development Committee inquiry into community violence", reported in the *Herald*, 29 August 1988.

19. Social Development Committee Inquiry into Community Violence, reported in the *Herald*, 29 August 1988.

20. The Federation of Community Legal Centres, "Police responses to domestic violence since the introduction of the *Crimes (Family Violence) Act*", interim paper, Melbourne, 1990, p. 3.

21. The Federation of Community Legal Centres, *A Long Way to Go — Police Response to Domestic Violence 1991/92*, May 1992, p. 1.

22. Wearing, p. 279.

23. B. Naylor and D. Neal, "Preventing domestic killings", *Legal Service Bulletin*, vol. 15 no. 3, June 1990, p. 101.

24. M. Warren, "Police response to family violence in Victoria", paper delivered to the 2nd National Conference on Violence, Australian Institute of Criminology, 1993.

25. Hatty, *Male Violence*,.p. 82.

26. Hatty, *Male Violence*, p. 83.

27. Law Reform Commission of Victoria, "Homicide prosecutions study", appendix to *Report No. 40: Homicide.*

28. Hatty, *Male Violence*, p. 51.

29. Hatty, *Male Violence*, pp. 68–9.

30. Wearing, p. 59.

31. Former Community Policing Squad Co-ordinator Bob Lovell, quoted in C. Nagle, "Violence in the home", *Police Life*, 16 October 1987, p. 2.

32. Wearing, p. 281.

33. Wearing, p. 289.

34. *Herald*, 9 September 1988, p. 4.

35. Federation of Community Legal Centres, "Equality before the law — access to justice. The discrimination faced by women from non-English-speaking backgrounds", submission by the Violence against Women and Children Working Group to the Australian Law Reform Commission Equality before the Law Reference, October 1993.

36. Inspector R. Baker, "Domestic violence and police powers", paper presented at Human Resource Centre Conference, 26–7 July 1982, p. 26.

37. Assistant Chief Commissioner Green, Victoria Police, 3 September 1988.

38. Hatty, *Male Violence*, p. 106.

39. Naylor & Neal, p. 99.

40. B. Naylor, "The Law Reform Commission of Victoria homicide prosecutions study: the importance of context', *Homicide: Patterns, Prevention and Control*, proceedings of a conference held 12–14 May 1992, AIC.

41. Homicide prosecutions study.

42. Wearing, p. 56.

43. Wearing, p. 57.

44. W. Bacon and R. Lansdowne, "Women who kill husbands: the battered wife on trial", in C.O'Donnell and J. Craney (eds), *Family Violence in Australia*, Longman Cheshire, Melbourne, 1982.

45. Elliott & Shanahan, p. 129.

46. Wearing, pp. 54 & 74; see also M. Dimopoulos and H. Assifiri, "Migrant woman as deviant", paper presented to the Multi-Culturalism and the Criminal Justice System Conference, Melbourne, May 1993.

47. Dimopoulos & Assifiri.

48. National Committee on Violence against Women, submission to the Joint Select Committee on Certain Aspects of the Operation and Interpretation of the *Family Law Act*, December 1991, p. 20.

49. National Committee on Violence against Women submission, p. 21.

50. Elliott & Shanahan, p. 125.

51. Elliott & Shanahan, p. 119.

52. National Committee on Violence against Women, *The* Family Law Act 1975: *Aspects of its Operation and Interpretation*, Australian Government Publishing Service, Canberra, 1992, p. 212.

53. Quoted in *Women's Services Report 1992*, Women's Services Coalition.

Chapter 5 — After the killing — the legal system

1. *Homicide: Report 40*, pp. 18 & 19 refer to their prosecutions study, which found that in half of domestic murder cases, witnesses told police of previous domestic violence. Their interpretation of this data was that there was probably more previous violence but the witnesses did not have knowledge of it. An alternative or additional interpretation is that the police did not interview witnesses about this history.

2. *Sunday Herald*, 15 July 1990.

3. One study of women who killed their husbands found that the actual questions asked by police influenced outcomes. The questions they looked at were "limited by a concentration on the issues that will be relevant in the trial, specifically intention, and by the policeman's own personal prejudices and preconceptions". The study concluded that "Unless s/he [the police officer] is alive to the possibility that the woman has been beaten by her husband and sympathetic to a woman in that situation, evidence of such beating may not appear in the record of interview simply because the right questions were not asked": Bacon & Lansdowne in O'Donnell & Craney, pp. 87–8.

4. *Homicide: Report 40*, p. 42.

5. *Sun,* 10 July 1990.

6. *Zekavic*, 1987.71, Australian Law Reports, p. 641.

7. *Homicide: Report 40*, p. 47.

8. *Sun,* 31 May 1989.

9. J. Scutt, *Women and the Law*, 1990, The Law Book Company, Sydney, p. 463.

10. *Age,* 5 December 1988.

11. *Homicide: Report 40*, p. 78.

12. For more information we suggest S. Tarrant, "Provocation and self-defence: a feminist perspective", *Legal Service Bulleti n*, vol. 17 no. 1, 1992, pp. 39–41; Bacon & Lansdowne in O'Donnell & Craney, pp. 67–94.

13. E. Sheely, J. Stubbs, J. Tolmie, "Defending battered women on trial: the battered woman syndrome and its limitations", *Criminal Law Journal*, 1992, vol. 16 no. 6, p. 369.

Chapter 6 — Media complicity in murder

1. Jane Cafarella, *Age*, 3 August 1990.
2. R. Davies, J. Dickey, T. Stratford, (eds) *Out of Focus: Writings on Women and the Media*, Women's Press, London, 1987, p. 2.
3. *Sun*, 4 September 1990.
4. *Age*, 23 March 1993.
5. *Herald*, 9 September 1988.
6. 29 August 1989.
7. *Guardian Weekly*, 4 November 1992.
8. See, for example the *Sun*, 10 July 1990, the *Herald-Sun*, 1 November 1991.
9. Lovejoy, 1979.
10. H. Kiel, "Partners in crime", *Legal Service Bulletin*, vol. 14 no. 6, 1989, p. 254. Also P. Grabowsky and P. Wilson, *Journalism and Justice — How Crime is Reported*, Pluto Press, 1989, p. 9; *The Families of Mark Militano*, Flemington/Kensington Community Legal Centre; *You Deserve to Know the Truth: Police Shootings in Victoria*, 1987 Fitzroy Legal Service, 1992, p. 82.
11. *Sun*, 29 November 1990.
12. *Age*, 8 July 1990.
13. *Age*, 15 July 1990.
14. *Sun*, 13 January 1991.
15. *Age*, 30 November 1988.
16. *Age*, 30 November 1988.
17. *Sun*, 4 July 1990.
18. *Age*, 4 July 1990.
19. "Husband used for a passport", *Sun*, 27 March 1990.
20. *Sun*, 4 July 1990.
21. *Age*, 8 July 1990.
22. *Sunday Age*, 15 July 1990.
23. *Sun*, 4 June 1990.
24. *Sun*, 3 March 1989.
25. *Northern Star*, 1 November 1978.
26. *Sun*, 14 September 1959.
27. *Sun*, 23 October 1990.
28. *Sun*, 12 August 1989.
29. *Sun*, 5 October 1990.

30. *Sun*, 15 September 1989.
31. *Sun*, 14 March 1984.
32. *Sun*, 4 July 1990.
33. *Sun*, 10 July 1990.
34. *Sun*, 15 September 1989.
35. *Age*, 4 November 1990.
36. *Sun*, 5 September 1990.
37. *Sun*, 6 September 1990.
38. Davies et al., 1979:4.
39. *Sun*, 3 November 1990.
40. *Sun*, 31 October 1990.
41. *Sun*, 20 November 1990.
42. *Sun*, 2 November 1990.
43. *Sun*, 14 August 1991.
44. *Sun*, 8 November 1990.
45. *Sun*, 28 Febraury 1989.
46. *Sun*, 16 October 1990.
47. *Ballarat Courier*, 1 May 1990.